Is AI Good for the Planet?

Digital Futures Series

Is AI Good for the Planet?

BENEDETTA BREVINI

polity

First published in 2022 by Polity Press

Polity Press
65 Bridge Street
Cambridge CB2 1UR, UK

Polity Press
101 Station Landing
Suite 300
Medford, MA 02155, USA

ISBN-13: 978-1-5095-4794-4
ISBN-13: 978-1-5095-4795-1(pb)

A catalogue record for this book is available from the British Library.

Typeset in 11 on 15pt Adobe Garamond by
Cheshire Typesetting Ltd, Cuddington, Cheshire
Printed and bound in Great Britain by CPI Group (UK) Ltd, Croydon

For further information on Polity, visit our website:
politybooks.com

I have been inspired, shocked and challenged by the company of many scholars, environmental activists, artists and thinkers when writing this book. I am most grateful for the intellectual generosity of the people who have read portions of this manuscript and supported me on this journey. First and foremost my wonderful friend and editor in chief, Fiona Giles, whose literary and academically rigorous comments helped to keep me focused, at a time when the world seemed to be falling apart during the pandemic. I am also grateful to a group of women who are a constant inspiration to me, for their activism, strength and integrity: Vicky Mayer, Alana Mann, Priscilla Karant, Terry Woronov, Lyn Hsieh, Sarah Gong, Lucia Sorbera, Laura Forlano, Melinda Rankin and Felicity Ruby. I am grateful for the feedback I received from Graham Murdock, and our constant exchanges – Graham is the best mentor in the world. I'm also grateful to Frank Pasquale for our numerous conversations on AI, public interest and our beloved political economy. My unbounded thanks to

Acknowledgements

Mary Savigar at Polity Press for believing in this project since its start and whose thoughtful comments helped bring the manuscript to life. Finally, a special thank you to my family, for the love I always received and for giving me the strength, values and determination to always fight for a more just world.

Introduction

Imagine sitting at your desk during one of those long COVID-19 lockdowns and remotely controlling a cartoon-like character that has your features. You've given her your name and move her through the big Piazza del Duomo in Milan – yes, just beside la Galleria – so she can buy that cool dress for you by Dolce & Gabbana that you've been dreaming about for ages.

This isn't a video game. It's your cheaply rented humanoid robot shopping for you, trying on clothes for you, giving you the best advice on colour combinations on the basis of your thousands of previous Google searches, then even mailing your purchase to your home address. And next, you send your robot-you to visit your mum, to keep her company until you have time to call her for a live video stream conversation. Meanwhile your robot-you sends your mum your favourite poetry, which your robot knows better than you do, thanks to the algorithm that revisits your YouTube and Netflix feeds.

We often think of artificial intelligence (AI) as a thing of the immediate future. This is hardly surprising, because we are constantly bombarded by slogans of AI coming to change our life, whether we like it or not. We are reassured it will be a better life. A better capitalism. A better environment. But AI is already here, and perhaps many of you didn't even notice – since many AI applications are already so embedded in our everyday life they no longer capture our attention.

Think of the AI-enabled camera that helps control traffic at the next intersection you cross. Or the facial recognition scan that you are forced to go through when you are at the stadium entrance. Think of all the latest smart phone applications, all running a variety of AI programs, when you are recommended music videos on YouTube, or when the Facebook app on your mobile scans your newsfeed in search of fake news, until you go home to your Google Home and Amazon Alexa.

But there is much more. AI technologies are translating languages, advising corporations on investments, flying drones, diagnosing diseases, protecting borders.

Fancy a social bot to overcome loneliness? Microsoft's Xiaoice (pronounced Shou-ice) chatbot recently became a global phenomenon with over 660 million international users and a reach of over 450 million smart devices (Zhang 2020). Xiaoice, which means 'Little Bing' in Chinese, was launched in 2014 by a small team of researchers and has since gained notoriety as a 'virtual

'If we lose our environment, we lose our planet and our lives. We must understand and debate the environmental costs of AI.'

girlfriend' across China, Japan and Indonesia. Presented as a teenage girl, Xiaoice is built on an empathetic computing framework that enables machine recognition of feelings and states, allowing dynamic responses; and this results in an AI companion with high emotional intelligence, which encourages long-term connections with its users.

There is also a significant amount of research connecting AI systems to applications in medicine. An international study examining the potential use of AI in the field of dermatology has found improved diagnostic accuracy and clinical decision-making when AI is used in conjunction with human clinical checks, suggesting stronger results than the use of AI or experts alone (Tschandl et al. 2020). The artificial neural networks analyse uploaded pictures and identify potential sites of malignant melanoma; this is currently being tested in an Australian skin clinic. The program has since been able to recognize melanoma at sizes smaller than the human eye can detect, for instance melanomas as small as 0.2 millimetres (UQ News 2020).

This is without mentioning AI's current applications in the global conservation field – from modelling biodiversity loss to monitoring migratory species and climate change scenarios. AI's emerging use in agriculture has aimed to optimize everything from crop production to resource consumption, harvesting, monitoring and processing. In 2019, twenty-five European countries signed a declaration of cooperation for the digitalization of agriculture, in an acknowledgement of the potential power of digital technologies and with the goal to establish infrastructure designed to support a smart agri-food sector (European Commission 2020a). Projects funded by the European Union (see Brevini and Murdock 2017) include Sweeper, a sweet pepper-harvesting robot that uses algorithms for fruit detection and localization and that was the first of its kind to demonstrate harvest success in a commercial greenhouse (Arad et al. 2020).

Or take CORaiL, an AI-powered solution to monitor and analyse coral reef resilience. Since May 2019, it has been deployed in the reef surrounding Pangatalan Island in the Philippines and has helped researchers to study the effects of climate change in the area (Wu 2020). Another famous robot wandering around the Great Barrier Reef in Australia is called LarvalBot and designed to carry coral larvae across destroyed areas of the reef. The larvae are distributed so that new coral colonies can form and new coral communities can develop. This process mitigates the damage caused by mass bleaching, weather events and climate change (Cimons 2019).

Some of these AI technologies are simply processing the data according to a basic set of formulae. Others are more complex systems that are effectively able to teach themselves progressively and learn from data as they are collected.

Despite the different complexities and endless applications, the dominant rhetoric around AI extends far past its current capabilities. Accounts across countries throughout the world proclaim the imminent development of intelligent machines, capable of outsmarting the human mind, amid promises to change everything fundamentally, from our working lives and domestic habits to transport and health services – to name just a few areas that will be affected. In the last decade we have witnessed a clear increase in predictions that the arrival of superintelligence is imminent; thus nations are expressing an urgent need to be ready for AI. As Goode writes, this is leading to the 'sublime spectacle of inevitability . . . that does little to offer lay citizens the sense that they can be actively involved in shaping its future' (Goode 2018: p. 204).

AI is thus being promoted as the principal solution for many of humanity's challenges; it is put forward as inevitable and ineluctable (Brevini in press). The following statement, taken from the official communications of the European Union, could not be clearer: 'AI is helping us to solve some of the world's biggest challenges: from treating chronic diseases or reducing fatality rates in traffic accidents to fighting climate change or anticipating cybersecurity threats' (European Commission 2018b).

The High-Level Expert Group on Artificial Intelligence (AI HLEG) appointed by the European Commission goes into even greater detail about the capabilities of AI to make humanity 'flourish' by solving virtually all problems of society:

> We believe that AI has the potential to significantly transform society. AI is not an end in itself, but rather a promising means to increase human flourishing, thereby enhancing individual and societal well-being and the common good, as well as bringing progress and innovation. In particular, AI systems can help to facilitate the achievement of the UN's Sustainable Development Goals, such as promoting gender balance and tackling climate change, rationalising our use of natural resources, enhancing our health, mobility and production processes, and supporting how we monitor progress against sustainability and social cohesion indicators. (European Commission 2019a)

Consequently, when the artificial machine arrives in this future–present that is always inevitably imminent, it will manifest as a superior intelligence, capable of solving the problems that humans have created – and climate change *in primis*.

As citizens, we are almost left with the sense that this artificial entity that will come to rescue humanity, the world, and all living things is a divine, magic hand, a *deus ex machina*.

This portrayal of AI as a benevolent deity has a crucial effect: it obfuscates the materiality of the infrastructures and devices that are central to AI's functioning. In all its variety of forms, AI relies on large swathes of land and sea, vast arrays of technology, and greenhouse gas-emitting machines and infrastructures that deplete scarce resources through their production, consumption and disposal. AI requires increasing amounts of energy, water and finite resources.

Why are we not talking about the negative impact of AI on the climate crisis? This is precisely what I want to discuss in this book. And more: I want to bring the climate crisis to the centre of debates around AI developments.

Clearly there are other important concerns about AI developments, from moral and ethical appeals for caution in the use of AI in military operations to mounting fears in areas where human expertise is crucial to safeguarding human rights (such as public health and the judiciary). There are huge ethical issues concerning documented algorithmic racial and gender biases, and fears that AI will make human labour redundant, producing a class of supereducated employees and another of less educated, unemployable workers.

These concerns are beyond the scope of the present book. If we lose our environment, we lose our planet and our lives. So we must understand and debate the environmental costs of AI.

The COVID-19 global pandemic caused the worst economic contraction since the Great Depression. It underscored the need to rethink the type of economy and society we want to build as we face the worsening climate crisis. Bold green recovery plans have been announced all around the globe (European Commission 2020b), and we have been told that technological innovations and AI are at the centre of recovery, as they have the potential to create millions of jobs and to boost economies devastated by the pandemic. But what would happen if we discovered that the environmental impact of AI is so massive that it compromises the plans to decarbonize the economy proposed by Green New Deals around the world?

The climate crisis is here to stay

In October 2018, the world's leading climate scientists who comprise the Intergovernmental Panel on Climate Change (IPCC) warned the world that there were only twelve years for global warming to be kept to a maximum of 1.5-degree C (see IPPC 2018). Beyond that level, the risks of life-threatening weather events such as drought, wild fires, hurricanes, extreme heat and poverty for millions of people will be significantly worse. One need only look at the devastation of Australia's ecosystem by the bushfires in the summer of 2019 to understand the gravity of the situation.

In November 2019 we received even clearer warnings from the UN Emissions Gap Report 2019, which assessed the gap between anticipated emissions in 2030 and levels consistent with the 1.5°C increase in temperature outlined in the Paris Agreement (UN Environment Programme 2019). It is estimated by the IPCC that an increase in average global temperature beyond this limit will lead to loss of habitable land for many humans and other life forms, as well as to catastrophic water shortages and crop shortages; this will cause massive migration and possible conflicts, as populations seek safer ground. The UN report also explains that the national commitments made in Paris must increase at least fivefold if we are to prevent a temperature increase greater than 1.5°C. Unless emissions fall by 7.6 per cent each year in the period between 2020 and 2030, the world will miss the opportunity to limit the damage. We are currently on a trajectory for a temperature rise of over 3°C (UN Environment Programme 2019).

Unfortunately, even despite the lockdowns of 2020, greenhouse gas emissions have remained stubbornly high. Daily global carbon dioxide emissions fell by as much as 17 per cent in early April 2020. But, as the world's economy started to recover, emissions rebounded; and the UN showed that 2020 only saw a 4–7 per cent decline in carbon dioxide relatively to 2019 (United Nations News 2020). While transportation and industrial activity declined from January 2020, electricity consumption remained constant, which partly explains the minimal drop in emissions. How, you may ask? According to the *World Energy Outlook 2019*, globally 64 per cent of the global electricity energy mix comes from fossil fuels (coal 38 per cent, gas 23 per cent, oil 3 per cent: IEA 2019). Since fossil fuels are the largest source of greenhouse gas emissions, without fundamental shifts to renewable resources in the global energy production we shall not be able to prevent incalculable loss of life, as the planet becomes uninhabitable.

What is the connection, then, between the climate crisis and the energy used by AI?

The chapters of this book help readers to answer this question through a discussion of the following themes:

1   a definition of AI and its promises for the world and the environment;
2   why data capitalism is crucial to an understanding of AI and who controls and develops AI;
3   why AI worsens the climate crisis; and
4   what we can do about it.

In chapter 1 you will learn about the hype and awe of AI. From the European Union to the United States and China, governments and global consultancies are urgently signing declarations that promise that the effects of AI are comparable to those of previous scientific revolutions, such as steam and electricity. This belief that AI will rescue humanity, solve the climate crisis and reduce the inequalities of capitalism has a crucial effect: it obfuscates the materiality of the infrastructures and devices that are central to AI's functioning. Setting aside the mythical discourse on AI, chapter 1 aims instead to shed light on definitions of AI and asks you to think about AI in a different, more material way than most of us have done in the past.

In chapter 2 you'll discover why data capitalism is crucial to the development of AI. You will understand the reasons for AI's rapid adoption, since 2010, as a result of vast computing resources and oceans of data. From that time, pushed by digital lords of the West such as Google, Facebook, Amazon, Microsoft and Apple (Brevini 2020), AI has been adopted virtually by all businesses and already extends through almost every sector of the economy and society. This chapter also explores the gatekeepers of AI power and imperialism, from the United States to China, and concludes with an examination of lobbying efforts by the most powerful tech giants to set the terms of public debates on AI and to determine policy outcomes (Benkler 2019, p. 161).

In chapter 3 you will discover the environmental costs of AI and its relationship to the climate crisis. The converged communication systems upon which AI relies generate a plethora of environmental problems, starting with energy consumption and emissions, material toxicity, electronic waste and disposal (Brevini and Murdock 2017). As you will realize, AI relies on large amounts of data, since it works with unsustainable energy demands imposed by algorithm training and cloud computing. Finally, while promising to solve the climate crisis, AI companies are marketing their services to coal, oil and gas companies, thus compromising efforts to reduce greenhouse gas emissions and to divest from fossil fuels.

The Conclusion argues that without challenging the current myths of limitless economic growth and boundless consumerism, without reconsidering the way in which the structures, the violence and the inequality of capitalism work, we won't be able to achieve the radical change we need if we are to tackle the climate crisis. So, instead of embracing AI as a new utopia that will fix the world and solve the problems created by capitalism, we should start quantifying and reducing the environmental costs and damages of the current acceleration of algorithm-powered AI. After listing a clear set of practices and policy, including practical changes that are easily within our reach, the book argues that abandoning a limited ethics framework and embracing a green agenda for AI that puts the climate crisis centre stage should be our urgent priority.

ONE

Defining AI
Beyond the Hype

The promises of artificial intelligence

If you read and watch the news regularly, you are certainly familiar with the hype and awe surrounding artificial intelligence (AI). Quite likely you'll have heard of AlphaGo, the AI-powered Go player? In May 2017, the world proclaimed that a 'Godlike' AI player defeated the then world champion, Chinese teenager Ke Jie. The Google-designed DeepMind device was programed for playing the ancient Chinese board game Go.

No human had ever played Go better than Ke Jie, until he was beaten by this US AI-powered machine. The sensationalism that followed the match, as over 280 million people watched it live in China, was unprecedented. Commentators described the match as a 'Sputnik moment'[1] for the development of AI in China, a moment that accelerated investment in AI in order for China to overtake the United States (Lee 2018). AlphaGo used deep learning essentially to teach itself to play, on the basis of millions of Go positions and moves from games played by humans. This was the first, but certainly not the last time commentators have used space metaphors such as 'Sputnik moment' to describe the impact of AI.

If AI can beat humans at Go, perhaps it can save us from the world's biggest challenges – all the range from treating global diseases to averting the climate crisis?

In 2016, President Barack Obama's Executive Office published two reports that outlined a comprehensive national plan for AI in the United States. The reports were set as a priority for the administration; one of them was prepared by the new National Science and Technology Council. Both called for key stakeholder involvement not only from defence and intelligence services but also from the departments of commerce, treasury, transportation, energy and labour. The reports, produced, remarkably, in only six months, reaffirmed the enormous potential of AI. On the topic, President Obama employed another space metaphor to convey the idea that the stakes could not be higher: 'The analogy that we still use when it comes to a great technology achievement, even 50 years later, is a moonshot. And somebody reminded me that the space program was half a percent of GDP. That doesn't sound like a lot, but in today's dollars that would be $80 billion that we would be spending annually

'As the handmaiden of neoliberalism, AI has consistently been hailed as the magic wand to rescue the global capitalist system from its dramatic failures.'

. . . on AI' (Barack Obama, as quoted in Dadich 2016).

The following year, emphasizing the enormous promise of AI and galvanized by its enormous potential for surveillance and repression, the Chinese government released one of the most far-reaching plans for investment in AI. Released in 2017, this three-step program is working towards the goal of making China a world leader in AI by 2030, with an industry worth US$150 billion. The Chinese government outlined strategies designed to support and promote the increased adoption of AI in various industries, in the military and within smart cities, and invested US$2.1 billion alone in an AI-focused technology research park. Complementing all this, the 2019 Beijing AI Principles were developed shortly afterwards, within a multistakeholder coalition (see 'In the struggle for AI supremacy, China will prevail', 2018; Roberts et al. 2019).

Besides the United States and China, many countries in the northern hemisphere have invested heavily in funding for AI technologies and intellectual property. France, Israel, the United Kingdom, South Korea and Japan have all joined the race for AI (Cognilytica 2020).

Although Europe is hardly considered a leader in AI developments, it, too, has invested significantly in AI technologies and employs the same enthusiastic rhetoric. In April 2018, the European Commission (EC) presented the 'Declaration of Cooperation on AI' signed by all 28 Member States of the EU including Norway. On 7 December 2018 the EC published a coordinated action plan on the development of AI in the European Union (European Commission 2018a, 2018b). It pledged to increase its annual investments in AI by 70 per cent, under the research and innovation program Horizon, in order to reach €1.5 billion for the period 2018–2020.

In evocative terms, the EC report emphasized the revolutionary character of AI, declaring the latter comparable in this respect to other scientific transformations, such as the steam and the electricity revolution. 'Like the steam engine or electricity in the past, AI is transforming our world, our society and our industry. Growth in computing power, availability of data and progress in algorithms have turned AI into one of the most strategic technologies of the 21st century' (European Commission 2018b). Similarly, the Organisation for Economic Co-operation and Development (OECD), in a document it released before adopting the OECD Principles on Artificial Intelligence, stressed that AI

contributes to better lives and helps people make better predictions and more informed decisions.

These technologies, however, are still in their infancy, and there remains much promise for AI to address global challenges and promote innovation and growth. As AI's impacts permeate our societies, its transformational power must be put at the service of people and the planet. (OECD 2019)

In June 2019, the G20 adopted human-centred AI principles that draw from OECD's AI principles, envisaging major benefits to society. Such benefits are supposed to include solutions to the world's inequalities: 'The benefits brought by the responsible use of AI can improve the work environment and quality of life, and create potential for realizing a human-centered future society with opportunities for everyone, including women and girls as well as vulnerable groups' (OECD 2019).

It's impossible not to see, in this utopian discourse employed globally, the same rhetoric of the technocrats of the 1990s (Shirky 2008), who argued that the new communicative opportunities provided by the internet would usher in a new era for democracy and freedom (Gilder 2000; Negroponte 1998) and the end of history (Fukuyama 1992). The same ideological discourse, replicated in current techno-enthusiast claims about the cloud (Nye 1994), was more recently debunked by

Mosco (2014) in his book *To the Cloud: Big Data in a Turbulent World*. In pure Enlightenment tradition, this absolute faith in technology, embraced and supported by cybertarians, Silicon Valley circles, global consultancies and politicians (Dyer-Witheford 1999; Brevini and Swiatek 2020), turns into a powerful apology for the status quo and for the current structure of capitalism, without leaving any real space for critique.

Global consultancies promise: Automating industry, boosting profits

This unfailing rhetoric of optimism is amplified by the major global consulting companies' forecasts. This is unsurprising. Potential applications for machine-learning systems and automation are vast. However, in the realm of retail and manufacturing, these will come at the expense of workers, clients and contractors. The same rhetoric is also echoed by consultancies and service providers that work alongside the corporate and government policy sector. Rao and Verweij (2017) described AI as a transformative force for the global economy with potential impacts on productivity, GDP and economic gains. According to them, AI could increase product variety, personalization, attractiveness and affordability and by 2030 would derive 45% of economic gains from the stimulation of consumer demand.

Maximizing profits through AI: From the United States to China, excluding the developing world

As noted above, global consultancies tend to cast AI in a positive light, while downplaying any negative consequences. Companies tend to emphasize that AI will deliver massive revenues, essentially in three major ways: by boosting productivity and efficiency gains; by reducing labour costs (this is especially true for manufacturing and transport); and by raising the production of AI-powered services that in turn will encourage uber-consumerism. According to a team at the McKinsey Institute, supply chain management is one of four business operations earmarked for presenting the greatest potential for productivity gains through AI, the others being manufacturing, risk management and product development (Bughin et al. 2018). This assessment expresses the same expectations as the OECD, which in its *Digital Economy* report describes how AI will significantly cut costs and optimize the use of production factors and the consumption of resources in every sector of the economy (OECD 2020). The report 'AI: Built to Scale', by Accenture (2019), also demonstrated that this is clearly the same positive sentiment of most technology CEOs: 84 per cent of business executives believe that they need to use AI to achieve their growth objectives.

This belief in AI as a means to solve problems is also reflected in the proliferation of scientific and scholarly papers devoted to this subject. According to a 2020 report by the World Intellectual Property Organization (WIPO), the number of scientific papers in the field of AI has soared since 2000, and this was followed by a spike in patent applications between 2013 and 2016 (World Intellectual Property Organization 2020). The phenomenon points to a shift from theory to application, as AI seeps into production and learning through its artificial neural networks. The WIPO report found that the most popular patents were in the fields of medicine, transport, telecommunications and interactive personal devices, while growth areas included finance, agriculture, e-government and smart cities.

Another trend highlighted by the WIPO is the growth in patents registered by China, which in 2014 recorded its highest volume of first-patent filings. In the same year China, the United States and Japan, together, accounted for 78 per cent of all patent filings. This is in stark contrast to the situation that prevailed earlier in the century, when European countries dominated patent registrations, accounting for nearly one in five filings between 2000 and 2015 (World Intellectual Property Organization 2020).

Global consultancies emphasize AI's benefits not only for particular stakeholders, but for the world more broadly. They foster the notion that AI provides 'global benefits' that can be spread across the world; of course, the United States and China were expected to gain the most. Meanwhile, the ability of what is called 'the global South' to access these benefits remains less clear. In chapter 2 I will sketch out how the biggest corporations of AI serve to illustrate this point, and I will do so by considering the massive advantage that Silicon Valley and the Chinese digital giants have over newly emerging start-ups. The absence of infrastructure crucial to AI development is most profound in the poorest Latin American and African countries. While the lack of resources locks these countries out of AI gains, their economies have the most to lose from AI's uptake. They have populous workforces of low-income manufacturers and farmers who are most easily displaced by automation. Both China and the United States have announced massive investments in AI in the global South, in a way that some may argue resembles a neocolonial approach.

Why techno-solutionism will not fix the world: AI as 'mover' of capital accumulation

Despite all AI's predicted benefits to society, it is clear that its primary purpose is to maximize profits. As another McKinsey report states bluntly, 51 per cent of all the work done in the US economy could be automated, saving companies a sum of US$2.7 trillion, which represents an equivalent loss in workers' salaries (McKinsey & Company 2017). Moreover, the report predicts that AI could automate roughly a half of all the work globally by 2055. The COVID-19 pandemic has seemingly accelerated the process towards automation. History shows that, since 1990, every recession has been followed by a recovery that offered fewer jobs for the population affected by it. This time, as AI reshapes the workforce, we may end up with something more radical. Katharine Dempsey (2017), writing in the *Nation*, shares an analysis from Joshua Bengio, one of the world's eminent experts in deep learning: 'AI will probably exacerbate inequalities, first with job disruptions – a few people will benefit greatly from the wealth created, [while] a large number will suffer because of job loss – and second because wealth created by AI is likely to be concentrated in a few companies and a few countries.' In chapter 2 I will further show

how the companies that have a massive competitive advantage through AI are, of course, the tech giants. This is a set that I named 'digital lords'.

Instead of expecting AI to solve all society's problems, we should expect, as David Harvey (2005) puts it, that technology becomes 'a prime mover' of capitalist growth. In other words, technological 'fixes' have historically been developed to remove barriers to capital accumulation, not to address inequalities.

Falling in love with technological determinism

The technological deterministic argument that technology will fix capitalism and reduce its intrinsic power to exacerbate inequalities of income, race and gender is far from new (Negroponte 1998; Gilder 2000). In Mosco's words, '[o]ne generation after another has renewed the belief that, whatever was said about earlier technologies, the latest one will fulfil a radical and revolutionary promise' (Mosco 2005: 8; Brevini in press). Mosco rightly reminds us of James Carey's work, which discussed how machines have often been framed as employing a powerful religious ethos: 'in contemporary popular commentary and even in technical discussions of new communications technology, the historic religious undercurrent has never been eliminated from our thought' (Carey 1992: 18).

As a result, techno-solutionism is presented as a seductive means to solve complex social problems and to lift the global capitalist system out of its recurrent crises. It promises that virtually anything can have a technical and technological fix (Kurzweil 1985). The development of digital technology, we are assured, will empower people by getting rid of radical inequalities while naturalizing market-based solutions to every issue of governance. In his critique of technological determinism, Raymond Williams, one of the most respected cultural theorists to come from Britain, usefully defined it as a 'largely orthodox view of the nature of social change' (Williams 1974: 13. In a later publication he explained: 'The basic assumption of technological determinism is that a new technology – a printing press or a communications satellite – "emerges" from technical study and experiment. It then changes the society or sector into which it has "emerged"' (Williams 1985: 129).

But despite his belief in the opportunities offered by innovation, Williams also held that 'technology is always in a full sense social'. Thus its development and usage are always shaped by the social relations of the society in which it is adopted (see Williams 1981: 227).

In the 1970s and 1980s, when Williams was writing, the information revolution was just taking shape as a new dogma in government and corporate planning. It continued to be championed throughout the 1990s, being facilitated by the economic policies of Margaret Thatcher in Britain and Ronald Reagan in the United States (Dyer-Witheford 1999). Likewise, neoliberal principles of an unregulated free market economy have been closely aligned to the information revolution, being endorsed by corporate and governmental elites as the solution to the 'growth' crisis of the 1970s.

In the 1990s the neoliberal Clinton administration was an aggressive supporter of the technocratic information revolution. In 1994 Congress passed the National Information Infrastructure Bill, which launched the famous worldwide information superhighway, championed at the time by Al Gore in numerous speeches around the world. Since its early phases of development, AI has underpinned these expectations by making evocative claims about the imminent creation of a machine capable of surpassing the potentials of humankind (Brevini in press; Natale and Ballatore 2017; Elish and Boyd 2018). As the handmaiden of neoliberalism, AI has consistently been hailed as the magic wand destined to rescue the global capitalist system from its dramatic failures (Brevini and Swiatek 2020).

Recent studies of public debates on AI show the extent of the dominance of this technological deterministic ideology, especially in the United States (Mayer-Schönberger and Cukier 2013). For example, Elish and Boyd's research on AI rhetoric concluded that, 'through the manufacturing of hype and promise, the business community has helped produce a rhetoric around these technologies that extends far past the current methodological capabilities' (Elish and Boyd 2018: 58).

The promise to stop the climate crisis: An AI for the environment

The promise that AI will help to address the climate crisis is one of the most commonly reaffirmed pledges of AI. Certainly AI applications that enhance environmental management are growing at a rapid rate. In 2017, for example, a study conducted in the field of water management used artificial neural network and support vector regression (SVR) algorithms to predict reservoir inflows one month in advance, both in the United States and in China, with the help of climate phenomenon indices, local hydrology information and reservoir operation data (Yang et al. 2017). AI, together with deep learning and machine-learning models, has also been deployed to forecast adverse effects of future climate change on water resources. Analysing the conditions of a mountainous watershed in Northern China, AI methods identified climatological–hydrological relationships and projected future temperature, precipitation and streamflow along with annual hydrological responses to these variables (Zhu et al. 2020). The use of AI methods in Zhu and colleagues' study could enable informed water planning policy and localized climate change adaptation strategies.

In a similar vein, Treeswift, a spin-off from Penn Engineering, provides an AI-powered forest-monitoring system that uses autonomous drones and machine learning to capture data, images and inventory in order to map forest biomass. Treeswift can provide carbon capture data, deforestation monitoring, growth forecasting and support forest management with targeted applications across preservation, the timber industry and wildfire control (Lopez 2020).

There are claims that AI autonomous vehicles and electric cars will deliver reductions in greenhouse gas emissions; algorithms for eco-driving; ride-sharing; and the optimization of urban transport and traffic. AI is also predicted to assist in the integration and spread of renewable energy through ductile price mechanisms and efficient energy storage and load operation. By enhancing the productivity of the agriculture industry, AI is said to play a key role in resource management, to minimize the environmental impact of farming and to increase global resilience to extreme climate through various applications focused on data, on informed decision-making, and on augmented responses to changes in supply and demand (Mann 2021). This will be supported in part by the budding field of climate informatics, in which AI and deep learning networks are leveraged to revolutionize our understanding of weather and climate change. In the future it is expected that AI will transform the availability and accessibility of supercomputers. This would be particularly relevant to modelling simulations of climate and weather events and to analysing data in relation to natural disasters, as it will reinforce response coordination and preparation. Alongside augmented and virtual reality technologies, AI can also be leveraged in the creation of smart cities, where the automation of city management and of urban sustainability is maximized within an 'urban dashboard' that should process data on energy, water, traffic, people and weather. This dashboard could also be used to create a similar program for monitoring environmental systems and overseeing problems such as illegal deforestation, water extraction, fishing, poaching and air pollution. The 2018 World Economic Forum reiterated that the solution to the world's most pressing environmental challenges is to harness technological innovations – none more than AI. The report states: 'We have a unique opportunity to harness this Fourth Industrial Revolution, and the societal shifts it triggers, to help address environmental issues and redesign how we manage our shared global environment' (World Economic Forum, with PwC and Stanford Woods Institute for the Environment 2018: 3). The Forum also claims that AI will be the solution to the most pressing environmental problems, which it identifies as 'climate change, biodiversity, ocean health, water management, air pollution, and resilience, among others' (p. 3). In particular, the report referenced eight areas: autonomous and electric vehicles, energy, agriculture and food systems, climate informatics, disaster response, intelligent cities, a digital Earth and the reinforcement of science.

As I will show in chapter 3, major technology companies have joined the chorus of those who attempt to reinforce belief in the revolutionary potential of AI to solve the biggest environmental challenges of our time. One voice in this chorus is the program AI for Earth. Launched by Microsoft in December 2017, this is a five-year, US$50-million initiative that supports researchers and environmental groups through grants of Microsoft AI tools. The program calls AI a 'game changer' in the area of climate change.

In a similar vein, Al Gore, the former US vice president, highlighted the role of technologies such as AI in the fight against climate change. Echoing the cyberlibertarians of the 1990s, he said:

> we're in the early stages of a sustainability revolution. New innovations like machine learning, artificial intelligence and the Internet of Things are allowing for digital tools to help businesses be more sustainable . . . This sustainability revolution apparently has the magnitude of the industrial revolution, but the speed of the digital revolution. It is literally unprecedented. (Al Gore, as quoted in Debus 2019)

The connection with the claims of what has become known as ecomodernism (Asafu-Adjaye et al. 2015) is clear. Against those who place the unequal capitalist power relations at the centre of the climate crisis (Brevini and Murdock 2017; Foster 2002), the ecomodernist argues that technologies can fix the ecological crisis without the need to address the inherent environmental destructiveness of capitalism. Published in 2015, the ecomodernist manifesto was co-authored by a group of figures in the sustainability movement such as Nordhaus, Shellenberger, and Brand, all mainly associated with the Breakthrough Institute, a US think tank traditionally critical of environmental groups. The mantra of eco-modernism is that 'meaningful climate mitigation is fundamentally a technological challenge' (Asafu-Adjaye et al. 2015). In this way the necessity of limitless eco-nomic growth is not disputed but encouraged.

Ecomodernism has also found traction in leftist circles (Isenhour 2016), among those scholars who are of the view that 'the idea that the answer to climate change is consuming less energy – that a shift to renewa-bles will necessarily mean a downsizing in life – feels wrong' (Bastani 2017). For Bastani, a proponent of 'fully automated green communism', '[r]ather than consuming less energy, developments in wind and solar (and within just a few decades) should mean distributed energy of such abundance that we won't know what to do with it'. The International Kyoto Protocol on global warming, while designed to limit the greenhouse gas emissions of nations, has in fact further entrenched this attitude, encouraging many environmental advocates in the United States (including Al Gore in his presi-dential campaign of 2000) to push for technological improvements in energy efficiency in order to avert environmental disaster (Foster 2001, 2002).

This view, which we similarly find in cybertarian Silicon Valley circles, turns into a powerful apology for the status quo and is embraced by the same corporate giants that traditionally opposed action on climate change.

Beyond the awe and hype, what exactly is artificial intelligence?

So far you have encountered the overhyped account of a mythical AI, which will come to rescue us and our planet.

But do you know exactly what AI is?

AI can be defined as the ability of machines to mimic and perform human cognitive functions. These include reasoning, learning, problem-solving, decision-making, and even the attempt to match elements of human behaviour such as creativity.

While AI research started in the post-Second World War years, it has taken decades to advance it to the point where AI became able to enhance pattern recognition and statistical analysis and acquired problem-solving capabilities (Roszak 1986; Haugeland 1989; Martinez et al. 2019). And limits remain.

Despite its long maturation, research has not been able to recreate anything remotely comparable to human intelligence. In fact, most of the research funds and corporate investments are spent on what has been described as 'narrow AI' (Martinez et al. 2019), which remains hyperspecialized in carrying out a single task or solving a single problem. In short, these types of AI follow algorithms that abide by a set of instructions. At the opposite end of the spectrum sits 'general AI' (also known as 'strong AI'), which promises to achieve the heights of human intelligence (Martinez et al. 2019). But, depending on the technologist one asks, we seem to be either years or months away from creating such AI systems.

So, for example, the common voice assistant Siri or Google Assistant are examples of narrow AI, just like the millions of AI applications that make it possible for enormous volumes of data to be analysed. Think of street smart cameras, sensors, or GPS fitted in vehicles that generate tons of data. Narrow AI makes sense of these data, so that self-driving cars can navigate through traffic and sense obstacles in a road. Facial recognition, recommendation systems, translation, as well as smart and interactive robots, drones, medical equipment and weapon systems are all examples of narrow AI.

It is also useful to clarify the relationship between AI, machine learning and deep learning, as these terms are often used interchangeably.

While the post-Second World War era saw rapid developments in AI, machine learning was not commonly used before the late 1970s and had an accelerated growth in the 1980s (Crawford et al. 2016; Crawford and Calo 2016).

Here is an image that visualizes the distinction between them:

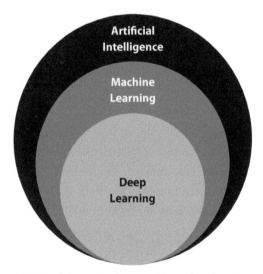

Figure 1.1: Visual distinction between AI, machine learning and deep learning

Source: Created by author

The three concentric circles represent AI as the broad category: machine learning is a subset of AI, while deep learning is a subset of machine learning. Kavlakoglu (2020) offers one of the most relevant explanations of these crucial terms:

the easiest way to think about artificial intelligence, machine learning, neural networks, and deep learning is to think of them like Russian nesting dolls. Each is essentially a component of the prior term. That is, machine learning is a subfield of artificial intelligence. Deep learning is a subfield of machine learning, and neural networks make up the backbone of deep learning algorithms.

A common example of AI without machine learning is that of rules-based systems, such as chatbots used in customer service or expert systems used in medical diagnosis. These are a set number of statements with specific instructions of the type 'if this, then do that'. In this case, the machine does not learn by itself (so the case is not one of machine learning), but it performs a set of clear instructions with many applications, for example in healthcare.

Machine learning and deep learning

In machine learning, computers are programed to learn from data that are input without being continually reprogramed. This means that the machine constantly improves its performance on a task – for example, learning to recognize a pattern.

Deep learning is a subset of machine learning. The 'deep' element in 'deep learning' is not a reference to some deeper kind of understanding achieved by this approach; rather the 'depth' of the computational model is represented by the number of layers in it. In deep learning, the machine uses different layers to learn from the data and is capable of managing a bigger volume of data than in machine learning. This also means that deep learning requires a much bigger data set for the learning process to take place. The classic recommendation system used for example by Netflix, a system that knows which show you'll want to watch next, uses deep learning models.

However, deep learning comes at a significant price, as we usually cannot say clearly why it made a certain prediction. This generates major issues, especially in healthcare. To go back to the opening example in this chapter, the highest profile of the capabilities of deep learning was secured by the worldwide success of AlphaGo, which used artificial neural networks to identify the best moves with the highest winning percentages.

Artificial intelligence as material technologies: Machines, cables, dust, devices

So far I have focused on the ability of machines to perform human cognitive functions and to make sense of data sets.

But we need to understand more, and I ask you now to think about AI in a different, more material way than most of us have in the past.

The following definition serves as a good starting point, as it stresses the connection between AI, data and algorithms: 'AI is a collection of technologies that combine data, algorithms and computing power. Advances in computing and the increasing availability of data are therefore key drivers of the current upsurge of AI.' This definition has now been adopted in the latest White Paper on AI issued by the European Commission (2020b).

It is crucial that we recognize AI's strong relation to what Vincent Mosco (2017) called 'the next Internet', where the crucial components are the cloud, datafication[2] and the Internet of Things (IoT). This approach stands in the tradition of critical political economy of communication, in which communication systems (including AI) are approached as assemblages of material devices and infrastructures, capable of depleting scarce resources in their manufacturing, usage and disposal (Brevini and Murdock 2017). Applying this framework to the present book, one can understand AI as a set of technologies, machines and infrastructures that demand amounts of energy in order to compute, analyse and categorize. They use scarce resources in their production, consumption and disposal, exacerbating the problems of waste and pollution.

Understanding what AI is (Gates 2020) may be crucial if we, as a society, are to play a less passive role in its development and implementation. Policymakers and entrepreneurs tend to emphasize the benefits of AI and to gloss over its disadvantages. A deeper understanding of AI equips us to make a more reasoned assessment, which AI policymakers and entrepreneurs may overlook, as they continue to believe that it is vital for AI to remain at the forefront of scientific development.

TWO

Controlling AI

Understanding Data Capitalism

Data capitalism and AI:
The indissoluble marriage

Can you, for an instant, visualize the stars of the universe?

According to the World Economic Forum (WEF), in one single day we produce forty times more bytes of data than there are stars in the observable universe.

That's 44 zettabytes, or 44 × 1000.000.000.000. 000.000.000 bytes.

How can we possibly produce so many data? Where do these data come from?

The breakdown given by WEF when it calculated the world's digital data production in one day looks extraordinary (World Economic Forum 2019):

500 million tweets are sent;
294 billion emails are sent;
    4 petabytes of data are created on Facebook;
    4 terabytes of data are created from each connected car;

65 billion messages are sent on WhatsApp;
5 billion searches are made.

Artificial intelligence (AI) would not have reached the current stage of development were it not for the unprecedented collection, extraction, analysis and monetization of data as the basis for data capitalism. Let me explain why.

There have been a few scholarly interventions that have placed data centre stage and have used a variety of labels, from 'platform capitalism', put forth by Srnicek (2017) in a book of this title, to 'surveillance capitalism' in Zuboff's (2019) more recent eponymous book, which draws upon previous work by Gandy (1989) and by Foster and McChesney (2014) on the role of data and surveillance. The common themes of these works are that data have a crucial value and that data collection is highly unequal, tending to replicate existing power asymmetries in societies (Brevini and Pasquale 2020). Their authors also argue that extraction has a major bearing on the way in which corporations and governments behave.

Shoshana Zuboff's book in particular makes a few very important claims, which can help to explain the crucial connection between data capitalism and AI. In her book *Surveillance Capitalism* she traces the history of the unprecedented success of Silicon Valley's digital lords, especially from the late noughties onwards, with a specific focus on Google, which she rightly considers to be the founder of and inspiration for surveillance capitalism.[1] The key insight of Zuboff's book is to identify how the collection of massive quantities of data from citizens creates the capacity for ongoing surveillance to achieve unprecedented commercial gain.

Google's monetization of targeted advertising accounts for only a small part of Google's global success: it is Google's invention and perfecting of surveillance capitalism as a method and as a business model that have led to its world dominance. The importance of AI in building this success is crisply expressed in a statement made by Hal Varian – the economist who has been dubbed 'the Adam Smith of Googlenomics': 'Nowadays there is a computer in the middle of virtually every transaction . . . now that they are available these computers have several other uses' (Hal Varian, as quoted in Zuboff 2019: 66). Varian then identifies four such uses: data extraction and analysis; new contractual forms due to improved monitoring; personalization and customization; and continuous experiments.

Put simply, the great discovery of Google was that, by learning to track, store, scrape and analyse massive amounts of data concerning citizens' behaviours and consumers' choices and by applying its own in-house (highly confidential) algorithms to make sense of these data, it would make immense profits through this ubiquitous extraction. Zuboff calls the crucial surplus generated by these processes 'behavioural surplus' (p. 14).

I hope you can see now the unmistakable role of AI in data or surveillance capitalism: it is AI that allows for raw data to be converted into the companies' algorithmic products that are designed to predict the behaviour of users. This is the secret of the digital lords' success.

What we have witnessed since 2010 is this relentless data collection, which has become the new norm for doing business; and it is coupled with the last decade's progress in computational power and cognitive abilities. The more data are available, the easier it becomes to perfect AI and help the digital lords to develop increasingly sophisticated algorithmic programs. This in turn ensures greater profit for the company that develops AI.

The 'techniques' of data or surveillance capitalism spread quickly from Google to the other digital lords, who were sitting on conspicuous amounts of data – first among them Facebook, Amazon and Microsoft. As a result of identifying a huge market for citizens' data, behavioural surplus made its presence felt far beyond the digital world. Prediction products began to be sold to electoral campaigners (starting with Obama's presidential campaign in 2008) and spread quickly into

the intelligence community. From there, data capitalism became the new standard of doing business: if it
made the digital lords so powerful, it could certainly
make other corporations powerful as well. Telecom
companies, cable companies, and virtually every commercial sector – from retail to banking, from insurance
to tourism, from hospitality and health to education –
rushed to make use of AI-powered services, in the hope
of maximizing revenue. So here we are: AI has perme-
ated almost every aspect of our lives.

I think that the reasons why AI technologies attract
such immense capital, government support, and research
resources are becoming clearer by now. Corporations
and states are well aware that AI has the capacity to offer
crucial strategic advantages in ever-widening areas of the
economy, of politics and of private life, as our data are
digitized, commodified, stored and traded.

The most powerful AI companies in the United States

I am sure that, after this discussion about data capitalism as the engine for AI, you won't be surprised to learn
that the most powerful tech giants in the world are
also the leading forces of AI. Of course, it is the same

'The most powerful
tech giants in the world
are also the leading forces
of AI.'

corporations – Google, Facebook, Microsoft, Amazon, and to a certain extent Apple, as well as their Chinese counterparts, Tencent, Alibaba and Baidu – that exploit their immense advantage when it comes to access to data and technical computing capabilities.

Let's start with the United States, where, besides the most established giants, we can see also a few small but promising start-ups.

Since Amazon's beginnings in the 1990s, its business strategies have been characterized by an obsession with data extraction and customer profiling (Brevini and Swiatek 2020). As a result, Amazon has become what I have previously identified as a digital lord: an entity that systematically collects, matches, and evaluates users' behaviour on its own platform and beyond, in order to create an impressive database of profiles. But these data are also fundamental to feeding a number of other businesses, starting with the ones that manufacture the most successful products sold under the Amazon brands – products crucially tied to consumers' preferences. It is notable that third-party sellers on Amazon don't have access to their own customers' data but must purchase Amazon's. These profiles serve as important capital for Amazon's research and development and feed into all its AI expansions and Internet of Things (IoT) products (Brevini and Swiatek 2020).

Most of us already know Alexa, the 'face' of Amazon AI. But Amazon Web Services (AWS), Amazon's offering for businesses, also produces a set of machine-learning programs and AI services that boast over 10,000 customers – among them NASA, Netflix, Tinder and Siemens. Additionally, Amazon has employed AI massively in all its production and distribution chains. For example today, in 2021, it has more than 200,000 mobile robots working inside its warehouse network and 'fulfilment centres' (Brevini and Swiatek 2020).

Apple's AI development has the company's most emblematic symbol in Siri, its popular virtual assistant. However, the company's latest rush to buy tech start-ups, notably the fact that it paid US$200 million to acquire the Seattle-based AI company Xnor.ai, provides a glimpse into the company's thinking when it comes to future devices.

Facebook, as mentioned earlier, has been the second company after Google to embrace behavioural surplus and data extractionism as its core business. It has also invested heavily in AI research, signing partnerships with research centres and universities. Facebook's ten-year road map highlights clearly that its two crucial objectives during the decade 2016–2026 are to get more users on the platform and to use AI to boost engagement and targeting.

IBM was involved in the birth of AI in the 1950s and remains firmly committed to this technology. With Watson, IBM created a machine-learning platform that can integrate AI into business processes such as building a chatbot for customer support. In 2021 IBM has committed to investing US$2 billion to develop AI intelligence hardware and to boost its AI performance about one thousand times over the next ten years. IBM is also developing a partnership with the State University of New York to develop the AI Hardware Center at the university's Polytechnic Institute in Albany.

Nvidia is one of the oldest AI companies that still play an important role today. Its graphics processors are the be-all and end-all of machine learning and AI. This Delaware-based company is active in healthcare, higher education, retail and robotics. In the area of deep learning developments, Nvidia concerns itself with integrating AI at every level of vehicle manufacturing and autonomous driving.

When the Huawei CEO Richard Yu unveiled the world's first AI smartphone chip, Kirin 980, in 2018 in Berlin, the competition was intense. Kirin 980 can perform face recognition, object recognition, image segmentation, and intelligent translation at high speed. It has sparked a flood of other AI smartphone chips, and

HiSilicon, Huawei's chip manufacturer, significantly enhanced the second generation of AI chips.

Microsoft is involved in AI on both the consumer and the business sides, having purchased five AI companies in 2018 alone. Cortana, Microsoft's AI digital assistant, directly competes with Alexa, Siri and Google Assistant. AI features comprise a large part of the company's Azure Cloud service, which provides chatbots and machine-learning services to some of the biggest names in the business.

Like the other big players in Silicon Valley, Twitter, too, is committed to AI, especially given its endless acquisitions. Four AI companies have already been acquired; the most notable one is the Australian Magic Pony, purchased in 2016 for US$150 million. Magic Pony is developing machine-learning programs for visual processing on the web and on mobile devices; and, by using AI in the future, Twitter is likely to improve its systems of recommending specific tweets in users' timelines.

Intel has also been on a shopping spree, buying AI companies: it acquired both Nervana and Movidius, along with a selection of smaller AI start-ups. Nervana enables companies to develop specific deep learning software, while Movidius was founded to bring AI applications to devices with a deficient performance.

Intel is also working with Microsoft to provide AI acceleration for the Bing search engine.

Banjo is a smaller but still emerging player. The start-up was founded after the 2013 Boston Marathon bombing. Its genesis was in the use of AI to assist emergency services through real-time analysis of social media data. Banjo's investors, which have contributed US$120 million to date, include Japanese telco SoftBank.

While these companies are making significant strides in AI, they are all dwarfed by Google, the founder of surveillance capitalism (see Zuboff 2019). Google's acquisition strategy is uncompromising: this company buys every AI start-up it can reach. Meanwhile, Google's machine system TensorFlow has become free for all, along with its AI project, a chip installed in a device that facilitates the machine's learning. Sundar Pichai, Google's CEO, has already revealed that Google's long-term vision is evolving from a 'mobile first world' to an 'AI first world' in the computer industry (AI Business 2016).

One common central characteristic of AI development in the United States – and one that, in my view, aligns it with the Chinese development model – is the continuous and often non-transparent exchanges between academic research, start-ups in California and Massachusetts, and a vast network of projects funded by the US Department of Defense. In 2020, the United States announced huge investments for harnessing AI in many areas of the military, including weaponry, intelligence analysis, autonomous vehicles, logistics and decision-making. The Department of Defense's proposed budget for 2020 allocated US$927 million for AI, the competition from China being the alleged reason for its increase in expenditure.

Another field of rapid expansion in AI is the development of AI surveillance systems, a phenomenon that is far from being just an export from China. From IBM to Palantir, western companies are deeply involved in developing these programs (Arad et al. 2020) and in selling them beyond the western world. A report from the Carnegie Endowment for International Peace (2019) tracked a clear increase in the development of surveillance systems; such technologies are used in several smart city projects around the world to enhance real time control of residents, policing, facial recognition and border security.[2]

And what about the most powerful AI companies in China?

China's digital economy is gigantic. In 2019 it had an estimated US$1.5 trillion of online retail transactions, which is more than twice the volume of e-commerce in the US Center for Global Development (Lynch and Chung 2020). This is even more notable when we consider that China's Internet penetration rate (60 per cent) remains lower than that of the United States (87 per cent) (Statista 2020b). This immense online market has been closely protected by the Chinese government, so that China's domestic firms can flourish, while international competitors were banned – Facebook and Twitter in 2009, Google in 2010.

In 2017 China's State Council released a Next Generation Artificial Intelligence Development Plan (Roberts et al. 2019). The plan is a road map for using AI to upgrade the country's manufacturing and service industries so that China may catch up with the United States and other advanced economies. This is the latest in a long string of Chinese efforts to create an advanced technology ecosystem, less vulnerable to outside pressures.

Since the plan's inception, the Chinese government has actively pursued a strategy of developing a lively market, with AI platforms that rely heavily on China's three digital platform leaders or 'AI national champions' (Ding 2019; Jing and Dai 2017). These champions are businesses endorsed by the government and encouraged to focus on developing specific sectors of AI. For example, Baidu has been tasked with the development of autonomous driving, Alibaba with the development of smart cities, and Tencent with computer vision for medical diagnoses (Jing and Dai 2017; Ernst 2020).

Of particular interest is the active role of Chinese local governments. For example, the Alibaba Group and Foxconn have partnered with the city of Hangzhou for the City Brain project, which uses AI to analyse data from surveillance cameras and social feeds. However, as Dieter Ernst notes, 'a clear characteristic of this project seems to be a clear division of labour between the local government, which bears responsibility for broader aspects of traffic management, and the much narrower business objectives pursued by the Alibaba group, which, through its affiliate Ant Financial, uses facial recognition for payments at Alibaba-owned retail stores' (Ernst 2020: 21).

The start-up SenseTime is the current supplier of the facial recognition technology that the Chinese government uses to track its citizens. Its research team is studying deep learning at the University of Hong Kong, and its image recognition technology is known to be far ahead of the technology currently used by Google and Facebook. SenseTime's number one priority is smart vision technologies.

Another Chinese company, DJI, is still officially a start-up but has already been valued at US$15 billion. DJI has a market share of more than 70 per cent in the global drone market and is increasingly entering the AI market. The latest drones use AI and image recognition to avoid colliding with objects. DJI recently entered into a partnership with Microsoft for a drone-to-computer streaming project. Its entry into autonomous vehicles and robotics can be expected to happen soon.

Certainly the focus on enhancing military capability and economic growth is clear in China's broader AI strategy. As Roberts et al. (2019) note, China has the world's second largest military budget, with US$175 billion allocated in 2019 (on this, see Chan and Zhen 2019), but its spending is still only a third of the US defence budget. Several authors argue that China's investments in AI represent an opportunity to achieve breakthroughs in military technology in the now mythical race for dominance with the United States (Roberts et al. 2019).

China's AI strategy has shown that data arguably constitute China's primary AI advantage. Having relatively fewer obstacles to data collection and use, China has amassed huge data sets, which do not exist in other countries (Lee 2018). Of critical importance is China's significant cost advantage in big data management – a massive population of low-cost college students works long hours doing the repetitive work of categorizing huge troves of data needed to train algorithms (Lee 2018). Ernst's (2020) study of the alleged tech battle between the United States and China in AI chips shows an interesting development, crucial for AI. More specifically, Ernst (2020: 1) notes: 'It was assumed that China could always purchase the necessary AI chips from global semiconductor industry leaders. Until recently, AI applications run by leading-edge major Chinese technology firms were powered by foreign chips, mostly designed by a small group of top US semiconductor firms.'

However, as a testament to America's concern about China's threat to overtake the United States in technological omnipotence, the Trump administration sharply increased restrictions on China's access to US technology, especially semiconductors and software. Moreover, many hurdles were introduced to Chinese investments in 'sensitive' US firms, including the symbolic blacklist of companies that are barred from buying advanced semiconductors and software from US companies without the government's approval (Ernst 2020).

The 2010s will be remembered as a new era in the development of data or surveillance capitalism, a development on a breathtaking scale that the adoption of AI in the 2020s is continuously augmenting. As I will discuss in the next section, the increasing links between tech giants, governments and research institutes makes for a worrisome trend, which portends even greater consolidation of the giants' power to shape future developments in AI and its discourse.

Who controls AI controls the debate

As I have shown in chapter 1, the common narrative dominating debates about AI depict it as the battleground for global dominance and technological progress, with leadership in AI technology and systems hailed as the key marker of success ('China may match or beat America in AI', 2017). From the United States to China, world leaders are invested in making AI the business opportunity of the future – and thereby in selling it as a virtue and a public good.

This optimism about the possibilities and achievements of AI is fuelled by extremely effective lobbying efforts from the most powerful technology giants, which already dominate the market and the debate. From

Alphabet and Amazon to Microsoft, IBM and Intel, the giants of Silicon Valley are investing billions both in AI developments and in setting the terms of public debate on AI and thus determining policy outcomes (Benkler 2019: 161).

Major lobby groups go in to defend their vested interests in the policy arena, armed with publicly and privately funded academic research that vouches for the benefits and efficiency of AI. For example, we have many reports that Google lobbied fiercely in the United States, at the state and the federal level, for its right to put its self-driving cars on the road, after also enrolling Obama officials to lobby state regulators for crucial legislative changes (Ingrassia, Sage, and Shepardson 2016). Moreover, as Zuboff (2019) notes, both Google and Facebook currently lead aggressive state-level lobbying campaigns aimed at weakening regulations on biometric data and privacy protections.

A quick glance at the digital lords' lobbying efforts in Washington is revealing: as stated by Brevini and Swiatek (2020), over the past ten years seven digital lords led by Google, Facebook and Amazon are responsible for spending nearly half a billion US dollars on lobbying (Statista 2020b). These giants spend now on lobbying as much as, or more than, the banking, pharmaceutical and oil giants combined

(Brevini 2020); for example, Facebook's total expenditure on federal lobbying in the past ten years amounted to US\$81 million, while Google's total spending was US\$150 million.

The increasingly tight connections in AI research activities between tech giants on the one hand and research universities and institutes on the other are particularly troubling. For example, a report published in 2019 by the *New Statesman* revealed that in five years Google spent millions of pounds funding research carried out in British universities, including the Oxford Internet Institute ('How big tech funds the debate on AI ethics', 2019), while DeepMind, Alphabet's own AI company, has specifically supported studies on the ethics of AI and automated decision-making. Similarly, Facebook donated US\$7.5 million to the Technical University of Munich to fund new AI ethics research centres. Another concerning case is a US-based National Science Foundation (NSF) research program called 'NSF Program on Fairness in Artificial Intelligence' and co-funded by Amazon (see Benkler 2019). The digital lord has 'the technical, the contractual and the organizational means to promote the projects that suit its goals', as Yochai Benkler explains; hence 'industry has mobilized to shape the science, morality and laws of artificial intelligence' (p. 161).

The firing of the AI ethicist Timnit Gebru by Google is even more disturbing for the future of AI research (Tiku 2020). Her work has contributed to a broader understanding, in the tech industry, of the risk of structural racial bias in AI that can marginalize minorities and women, reinforcing existing structural inequalities.

How can academics working for the industry feel free to investigate major problems associated with AI, if the industry's interference in academic research becomes the norm? The dominance of a few tech giants in the field of AI has inhibited critiques about its development, while systematically avoiding a thorough discussion of the environmental costs of technology. A survey I conducted on AI strategy reports issued by different states in Europe shows how public debates on AI emphasize overwhelmingly positive aspects, which never consider the environment (European Commission 2019a, 2019b; Brevini in press). Concerns, where they are voiced, focus almost exclusively on the objective of delivering 'ethical AI' (European Commission 2019a), 'trustworthy AI' (European Commission 2019b) and fair or equitable AI – with AI itself always positioned as an inevitably public good. Thus a fundamental concern should be the total abdication of strategic decisions and choices on the direction of AI research and development, from government to corporate board-rooms. We continue to enable the privatization of public policy.

I move now to the central focus of the book, a point that is rarely mentioned by the most powerful players in AI: the massive environmental costs of AI.

THREE

Why AI Worsens the Climate Crisis

By now I have described the most popular applications of artificial intelligence (AI), the gatekeepers of AI power, and how AI is changing every aspect of our lives.

Let me now explain why AI is directly linked to the climate crisis.

Remember the case I mentioned at the end of chapter 2, of the dismissal of the AI scholar Timnit Gebru from Google (Tiku 2020)? Gebru is one of the most high-profile Black women data scientists and an influential voice in the field of ethical AI. At the centre of her sacking was a paper that Google clearly disliked, as it raised major concerns about certain AI models that are vital to its business (see Hao 2020). The paper is titled 'On the Dangers of Stochastic Parrots: Can Language Models Be Too Big?', and Gebru is one of its co-authors. This paper raises clear issues about the fact that AI models have become unwieldy and too data-intensive. It askes 'whether enough thought has been put into the potential risks associated with developing them and strategies to mitigate these risks' (Bender et al. 2021: 1).

Besides highlighting concerns about hate speech, biases and stereotypes, the paper is one of the few that also shed light on the environmental costs of AI and on how such costs disproportionately affect marginalized communities, which bear the brunt of climate change.

This story highlights once again how difficult it is to radically upturn the dynamics of a dominant discourse when the gatekeepers, those who control developments in AI, also exert immense ideological, economic and political power.

AI contributes to the climate crisis in several ways.

It continuously increases energy consumption in order to sustain the computational power needed for making sense of massive amounts of data and for training algorithms. It pushes to the limits the capacity of clouds and server farms, forcing the consequent demand for more electricity and water for cooling systems.

It boosts uberconsumerism, which in turn intensifies the environmental costs: first, consumerism intensifies the proliferation of unnecessary products and generates waste in packaging and through obsolescence; secondly, it promotes addiction to social connection through social media, a type of connection that requires more and more energy; and, thirdly, the collection of data designed to promote consumption generates even more data, thus adding to need for storage in clouds and server farms.

Additionally, the development of AI applications increases the costs of disposal of toxic and digital e-waste. Finally, as you will discover at the end of this chapter, AI is currently augmenting the efficiency of resource extractionism in both mining and agriculture.

For decades, ecological criticism has argued that the violence and inequities wrought by capitalism have ultimately caused the climate crisis we now face (Foster 2001, 2002). The accelerating impact of human interventions on the Earth's ecosystems identified in climate research coincides with the rapid expansion of communication and computational systems of the last decades (Brevini and Murdock 2017). This expansion has in turn drastically accelerated our consumption of raw materials and energy, compounding our global environmental challenges and exposing urgent questions of inequality and exploitation. As Andreas Malm and Alf Hornborg have noted, '[a] significant chunk of humanity is not party to the fossil economy at all: hundreds of millions rely on charcoal, firewood or organic waste such as dung for all domestic purposes', so that their contribution to greenhouse gas emissions 'is next to zero' (Malm and Hornborg 2014: 65). Nor is the 'the nearly one-third of humanity [with] no access to electricity' (p.65) making demands on energy consumption. This is why we need urgently to account for the costs and damages of AI specifically in relation to marginalized communities that don't contribute to or benefit from AI.

It is therefore vital that scholars quantify and measure the environmental costs and damages of the current acceleration of algorithm-powered AI, and that they also understand and counter the mythological machine that drives and protects its growth.

Computational power and algorithms

As mentioned in the Introduction, few studies have attempted to quantify the energy consumed by running AI programs. The first studies published in June 2019 by the College of Information and Computer Sciences at University of Massachusetts Amherst quantify the energy consumed by large AI language programs, and they do so with particular reference to a translation model (Strubell, Ganesh and McCallum 2019). Conducted by Emma Strubell and her collaborators, the study made an unequivocal, damning finding: a common AI training model in linguistics can emit more than 284 tonnes of carbon dioxide equivalent. This is comparable to five times the lifetime emissions of the average American car.[1] Considering that a flight between London and

Rome emits roughly 234 kg CO_2 and a return flight between London and New York City emits roughly 986 kg CO_2 (Kommenda 2019), the carbon emissions of this type of AI (at 284.000 kg CO_2) are roughly comparable to 288 return flights from London to New York City or 1,213 return flights from London to Rome. It should be noted that, given the perfecting of neural networks, which have been fed more and more data, the energy consumption of these large models and their carbon footprint have been exploding since 2017, which was the year under review in Strubell, Ganesh and McCallum's analysis.

Not surprisingly, the computational and environmental costs of training grew in proportion to the augmented size of the model; hence they increased when additional tuning steps were taken to increase the model's final accuracy. The concern is that machinelearning algorithms in general are consuming more and more energy, as they are using more data and training for longer periods of time (see Figure 3.1).

This trend has been corroborated by several studies that demonstrate how the amount of computing used to train deep-learning models has increased by 300,000 times in the six years between 2012 and 2018 (Schwartz et al. 2019).

Furthermore, as mentioned above, the converged

Comparing carbon footprint: carbon-intensive activities versus AI language models	
CONSUMPTION	**CO_2 (kg)**
Travel London–Rome (1 passenger)	234 kg CO_2
Travel London–New York City (1 passenger)	986 kg CO_2
American car average including fuel 1 lifetime	57152 kg CO_2
TRAINING ONE MODEL	
Natural language processing Development plus tuning	35592 kg CO_2
Natural language processing Transformer with neural architecture search*	284019 kg CO_2
*Transformer is a common type of deep-learning model introduced in 2017	

Figure 3.1: Comparing carbon footprints: Carbon-intensive activities versus AI language models

Source: Created by the author from data calculations in Strubell, Ganesh and McCallum (2019) and Kommenda (2019)

communication systems upon which AI relies generate a plethora of environmental problems of their own, most notably energy consumption and emissions, material toxicity, and electronic waste (Brevini and Murdock 2017).

Energy and data centre carbon footprint

The computing power necessary to train an algorithm is certainly not the only environmental cost of AI. The converged communication systems upon which AI relies generate a plethora of environmental problems of their own. This is because the systems use a tremendous amount of energy to manufacture the digital devices on which AI runs. They also rely on extensive energy-demanding infrastructure, adding significant costs that are based on energy consumption, emissions, material toxicity, and electronic waste (Brevini and Murdock 2017).

Artificial intelligence relies on data in order to work; and the need for data centres to increase their capacity and power has been steady in recent decades, as these centres house the thousands of servers that power various applications, analysing, organizing and automating a range of processes. Demand for their services has been rising not just steadily but rapidly, too; and precise data-intensive technologies such as AI, smart systems, manufacturing systems and autonomous vehicles promise to increase this demand still further.

At present, data centres eat up energy at a rate somewhere between the national consumption of Japan and that of India (Murdock and Brevini 2019; Greenpeace International 2011, 2017; Cook, Jardim and Craighill 2019): they average 200 terawatt hours (TWh) each year (Jones 2018; IEA 2017). This represents approximately

1 per cent of the total global electricity demand (Jones 2018). Estimates suggest that, by 2030, annual electricity demand from data centres could grow to as much as 8,000 TWh under worst case scenarios and 1,100 TWh under best case scenarios (Jones 2018). This is a lot of energy; moreover, one study by *Nature* estimates that in some countries this demand may reach somewhere between 15 and 30 per cent of the national electricity consumption – again, by 2030 (Kamiya and Kvarnström 2019).

In a time of climate crisis, the question of how we power global digital infrastructure is more urgent than ever. According to a major study conducted at McMaster University in Canada, the tech industry's carbon footprint could increase to 14 per cent by 2040, 'accounting for more than half of the current relative contribution of the whole transportation sector' (Belkhir and Elmeligi 2018: 448). This growth is so rapid that we need urgent action to change radically the way in which we power the tech industry.

As I spelled out in the Introduction, fossil fuel consumption is the leading cause of global climate change and creates other major environmental challenges. According to the International Energy Agency, globally 64 per cent of the global electricity energy mix comes from fossil fuels (coal 38 per cent, gas 23 per cent, oil 3 per cent: see IEA 2019), so it is paramount that fossil fuels are kept in the ground and we fully embrace renewable resources to produce electricity if we want to prevent global warming from exceeding 1.5°C by 2030 (IEA 2019).

If we compare data from the first report that Greenpeace International (2011) published with data from one of the more recent reports of the same organization (Greenpeace International 2017), we can see a significant increase in the prioritization of renewables among some of the largest internet companies that own data centres and are the biggest cloud providers.

The corporate world has been united in broadcasting its 'energy efficiency' achievements of the past five years. And it is certainly true that most of the improvements in emission reductions have been gained through decreased electricity consumption via data centres running in the cloud.

However, there are two caveats: first, we should be cautious about the tech giants' claims that their energy footprint is completely 'carbon-zero', since this result is achieved largely through carbon credits accounts operations. Secondly, the constant push to increase the capacity of cloud systems can easily compromise all efficiency gains: if the cloud grows faster than sustainable energy systems can replace fossil fuels, the cloud must receive more of its electricity from dirty sources (Amazon 2020).

For example, Microsoft claims that it has been carbon-neutral since 2012, but only by including its renewable credits (Microsoft 2020; Joppa and Herweijer 2018). In reality, its data centres run on 60 per cent renewable electricity, while the company plans to boost this figure to 70 per cent renewable energy by 2023. Similarly, in 2017 Google announced that it had reached its objective of using 100 per cent renewable energy across its data centres and operations, but in reality 40 per cent of this target comes from purchase agreements Google 2019). Google claims that all data processed via Google Cloud have zero net carbon emissions. However, many of its data centres are located in areas that are still heavily reliant on fossil fuels. The biggest cloud provider in the West, Amazon (see Amazon 2020; Brevini 2020), has recently promised to achieve net zero carbon emissions by 2040, but remains the weakest of the tech giants in its 'greening policies'. Greenpeace International reported that Amazon gave up its 100 per cent renewable commitment by expanding operations by 59 per cent, without renewable energy (see Cook, Jardim and Craighill 2019). In fact Amazon Web Services (AWS) continue to build significant data centre projects in locations where electricity is only

'Amazon has recently promised to achieve net zero carbon emissions by 2040, but remains the weakest of the tech giants in its "greening policies".'

based on fossil fuels. One of the most recent examples is Virginia, a state dominated by utilities that have little to no renewable energy, and one that therefore drives a dramatic increase in the consumption of coal and natural gas.

As noted in the Clicking Clean Report prepared by Greenpeace, major digital corporations' lack of transparency concerning their energy needs and the supply of electricity that powers their clouds remains the biggest threat to the greening of data centres (see Cook, Jardim and Craighill 2019, who describe the colossus of cloud's AWS, Tencent and Baidu as the least transparent in the world).

Additional environmental costs of data centres

There is another crucial form of energy consumption that data centres are responsible for: I'm talking about the energy needed to cool their systems. Data centres require large and continuous supplies of water for their cooling needs, raising serious policy issues in places such as the United States and Australia, where years of drought have ravaged communities and further imperilled biodiversity (Mosco 2017). As Evans and Gao (2016) from Google's DeepMind website explain,

> One of the primary sources of energy use in the data centre environment is cooling ... Our data centres – which contain servers powering Google Search, Gmail, YouTube, etc. – also generate a lot of heat that must be removed to keep the servers running. This cooling is typically accomplished via large industrial equipment such as pumps, chillers and cooling towers.

According to these authors, the solution to this problem is machine learning, which on the one hand can lead to efficiency savings, but on the other produces its own problematic carbon footprint.

Keeping data centres cool enough to allow applications to work efficiently is certainly a challenge. Some analysts have noted that analytics and machine learning are turning up the heat density of data centres another notch, so that the efficiency gains made a few years back are now reduced.

A lot of resources are currently employed to develop new technologies to solve the problems of cooling. One of the latest is the project by Microsoft to launch data centres on the ocean floor, which submerged 864 servers in saltwater (Roach 2020). One has to wonder what the environmental impact study found for a project on such a scale in the ocean.

Another issue that is rarely discussed when it comes to data centres is the progressive land clearing generated by the increasing demand for land for the construction of these massive hubs.

A typical data centre is an industrial building that provides floor space for housing information technology (IT) equipment, in addition to the necessary power distribution, cooling, cabling, fire suppression and physical security systems.

One of the biggest data centres in the world is the Utah Data Center, also known as the Intelligence Community Comprehensive National Cybersecurity Initiative Data Center, situated in Bluffdale, Utah and covering an area of 1.5 million square feet. Land clearing is an important part of the picture of environmental damage, as it reduces our planet's capacity to absorb carbon and it accelerates species extinction through the destruction of wildlife habitats. It also reduces the resilience of threatened species and their capacity to survive future crises, causing additional death and habitat loss (Nelder et al. 2017). The costs for local communities, animal and plant populations, and the atmosphere all need be taken into account, considering the emergency we are facing.

Artificial intelligence, uberconsumerism and waste

Recognizing the material presence of communication systems alongside their central role as key spaces of advertising and consumerism is essential to a complete account of the intersections between AI, communication systems, transformations in capitalism, and the escalation of the climate crisis.

As noted in chapter 2, the current modus operandi of capitalist economies promotes the consolidation and dominance of global tech organizations that function as digital lords (Brevini and Swiatek 2020). These giants reduce competition and impede innovation from smaller initiatives, thus interrupting the free flow of market forces, while at the same time they wield their inbuilt power to direct politics, the economy and uberconsumerism.

Artificial intelligence applications contribute to the production of an increasing range of commodities and services that can be sold to consumers and provide continuous opportunities to boost consumerism and advertising, taking them to new levels. It is certainly no secret that Facebook and YouTube profit when people stay longer on their sites; and they also profit by offering advertisers technology that delivers precisely targeted marketing. Data-driven communication systems have come to play an increasingly central role in geographically dispersed corporate and governmental activities, while the space available for advertising has significantly increased.

In addition to reinforcing the wastefulness of general overconsumption, new smart devices at the centre of everyday life add hugely to the climate crisis. This is due not only to the finite nature of the resources needed for manufacturing devices and their related consumer goods. The 'always connected' nature of internet of things (IoT) devices, tablets and smartphones significantly increases the demand for power supplies.

In 2019 the number of smartphones sold to consumers reached 1.52 billion units, a significant increase from the 680 million units sold in 2012. This means that over 19 per cent of the world's total population owned a smart device in 2019; and this figure is expected to increase by 37 per cent by 2021 (Statista 2020a).

The present assembly of digital machines and networks is the result of a long process of expansive proliferation, during which the opportunities to target consumers have expanded, too – and now they are multiplied by AI running on smartphone devices (Maxwell and Miller 2020). For example, smartphones have been at the forefront of efforts to develop 'frictionless' purchasing, bypassing cash and cards and encouraging consumers to swipe their smartphones across payment points. The intention is to increase the volume and rate of consumption in every corner of our life, keeping us connected to the applications for as long as possible and, in the process, generating more and more data to produce targeted advertising.

Consumerism is also pushed by digital media business models that have played a major role in accelerating the rates of product obsolescence and disposal by encouraging users to upgrade on a regular basis (Maxwell and Miller 2015, 2020). Older models are rendered obsolete through the withdrawal of spare parts and the ending of support for previous generations of software. The successive iterations of the iPhone embody perfectly this new, embedded rule of rapid replacement.

The ideology of consumer sovereignty deliberately fails to take account of the massive corporate investment in advertising and marketing that is devoted to sustaining and directing consumption, and the increasingly central role played by planned obsolescence in forcing consumers to upgrade or replace commodities on an accelerating basis, with devastating effect for the climate crisis. Apple's history of frequent, highly publicized product launches exemplifies digital media events that celebrate the short life-span of its products. As

Justin Lewis (2017: 58) noted, '[t]hese practices involve consumerist business models (notably planned obsolescence) and the promotion of a consumerist credo. They define progress in ways that rely on increasing rather than stabilising or decreasing global levels of production and consumption. In short, they operate to make catastrophic levels of climate change more likely.' Lewis concludes with a reflection that can be easily transferred to new AI applications: 'We are asked to measure progress entirely in consumerist terms: rather than evaluate the extent to which a new technology advances the human condition – either individually or collectively – we are encouraged to see progress as a conveyer belt of product upgrades' (p. 66).

Besides the increasing demand for power that I discussed earlier, the result of this acceleration is a mounting accumulation of electronic waste, much of it non-biodegradable and some of it toxic. A World Economic Forum review of available research estimated that there are currently over 150 million tonnes of plastic in the world's oceans and that, if business as usual continues, by 2050 oceans will contain more plastics than fish, by weight. Production of plastics will account for 20 per cent of total oil consumption and 15 per cent of the carbon budget needed to keep global warming below the internationally agreed level of 2 or

1.5 degrees centigrade (World Economic Forum 2016). Plastics are produced and disposed of in a number of other areas of economic activity, but the contribution made by communications sectors needs to be included in any full analysis of the connection between media technology and the climate crisis.

But there is more: AI is certainly one of the most successful drivers of this uberconsumerism and of business models based on continuous data extraction.

Together, the application of robotics and AI to productive processes and the IoT, which connects an increasing range of 'smart' domestic machines and devices to communication networks, generate an increasing body of data. This enables unabated consumption through the perfection of targeted advertising, consumerist business models, and the rampant nature of the current data capitalism, with its incessant demand for more resources and energy.

As I have discussed in chapter 2, the phenomenon of big data is at the core of AI's success. It is also, as previously explained, the reason behind the massive investments by tech giants into the development of AI. The more time we spend on Facebook on our digital devices, the more we depend on Alexa's instructions embedded in our smart home, the more data are collected to develop more AI systems. These in turn make us more dependent on devices that continually need updating, further degrading our connection to the environment and adding to waste.

AI runs on devices: The carbon footprint of information and communication technologies

If it is true that it takes a tremendous amount of energy to power data centres, consider the energy needed to manufacture, power and then dispose of the data-intensive technologies on which AI runs: smart devices, IoT, autonomous vehicles, distributed manufacturing systems, robots – to name a few. The energy footprint of the IT sector is already estimated to consume approximately 7 per cent of global electricity (Greenpeace International 2017). Data from the International Energy Agency show that global internet traffic surged by almost 40 per cent between February and mid-April 2020, pushed during the COVID-19 pandemic by growth in video streaming, video conferencing, online gaming and social networking. This growth needs to be considered in the context of the continuous demand for digital services over the past decade: since 2010, the number of active internet users worldwide has doubled, reaching almost 4.66 billion people as of October 2020 (Statista 2020a).

The number of mobile internet users is forecast to increase from 3.8 billion in 2019 to 5 billion by 2025, while the number of IoT connections is expected to more than double, going from 12 billion to 25 billion (IEA 2020).

What does this mean in terms of greenhouse gas emissions? The latest reports conclude that the information and communications technology (ICT) sector, which includes mobile phones networks, digital devices and television, accounts for something between 2 per cent and 3.7 per cent of global emissions (Jones 2018; The Shift Project 2019). This percentage is clearly much higher than that of the aviation industry, currently at 2 per cent and normally considered the biggest single culprit in driving carbon emissions.

The forecasts are also troubling: according to a recent study carried out at McMaster University in Canada, greenhouse gas emissions from ICT could grow from 1.6 per cent of the total global footprint in 2007 to 14 per cent by 2040 (Belkhir and Elmeligi 2018).

The impressive proliferation of online video has a massive bearing on this exponential increase in emissions linked to ICT – from consumption on demand (e.g. streaming, video on demand, cloud gaming) to high definition (HD) images. This proliferation is so great that the latest report by Cisco calculated that by

2022 the video-streaming traffic will represent over 82 per cent of the total consumer internet traffic (CISCO 2020).

In 2019 the video-conferencing global market was valued at $3.85 billion. Currently the growth rate of video conferencing has been substantially increased by the COVID-19 pandemic: 2020 has seen an unprecedented rise in the amount of video-conferencing. But video conferencing, often regarded as a greener alternative to face-to-face meetings, has an evident carbon footprint, generated by the energy it needs in order to operate. One study from 2012 estimated that a five-hour meeting held over a video conferencing call between participants from different countries would produce between 4kg (8.8lbs) carbon dioxide equivalent (CO_2e) and 215kg (474lbs) CO_2e, with variations depending on the quality and stability of the image (Ong and Cabañes 2018). By comparison, a trip from London to Rome has a carbon footprint of 234 kg CO_2 (as mentioned earlier). While video conferencing might produce a smaller carbon footprint than flying hundreds of people around the globe to a conference, it still generates a significant enough quantity of greenhouse gas to warrant consideration.

Energy and waste disposal

The constant increase in the sales of high-tech smart devices, sales that AI applications support and accelerate, combined with the planned obsolescence enabled by big tech companies, is generating vast problems of waste and disposal. Maxwell and Miller explained, in their groundbreaking work on the materiality of technology: 'Waste is a problem throughout the life cycle of any electronic device, from water over-used and contaminated in semi-conductor production to discarded solvents and other materials' (Maxwell and Miller 2017: 53). E-waste contains a list of harmful chemicals such as mercury, brominated flame retardants, chlorofluorocarbons and hydrochlorofluorocarbons, all of which may be released into the environment, harming human and non-human life in the areas where these materials are discarded. Such pollutants increase the mortality of local populations and bring about impairments of cognitive functioning and fertility. Like the effects of global warming, these harms are borne disproportionately by marginalized communities, as large amounts of e-waste are processed in low-income countries.

In 2019 alone, the world generated 53.6 million tonnes of e-waste. Asia produced the biggest share (24.9

million tonnes), being followed by the Americas (13.1 million tonnes) and by Europe (12 million tonnes), while Africa and Oceania generated 2.9 and 0.7 million tonnes respectively (Forti et al. 2020).

Unfortunately only 17.4 per cent of 2019's e-waste was formally collected and recycled, while the amount of undocumented e-waste is increasing. The Global e-Waste Monitor found that Europe has the highest collection and recycling rate, covering about 42.5 per cent of the total e-waste generated in 2019; Asia ranked second, with 11.7 per cent, the Americas and Oceania recycled 9.4 per cent and 8.8 per cent respectively, and Africa had the lowest rate, accounting for 0.9 per cent. So what happens with the remaining quantity – 82.6 per cent – of the world's e-waste?

Richard Maxwell and Toby Miller report that most digital waste produced in the United States is probably sent to Asia for recycling and dumping, but the Basel Action Network has revealed a trend of export denial in the recycling industry. Moreover, a portion of e-waste still ends up in mainland China, while much of the remainder finds its way to Pakistan, Thailand, Taiwan, Cambodia, the United Arab Emirates, Togo and Kenya (Maxwell and Miller 2020).

As the Global e-Waste Monitor explains, the improper management of e-waste not only creates a hazard to health but contributes to the climate crisis: if the materials in e-waste are not recycled, they cannot replace primary raw materials and reduce the extraction and refinement of greenhouse gas emissions. Next, the refrigerants found in some temperature exchange equipment are greenhouse gases. A total of 98 metric tonnes (Mt) of CO_2 equivalents were released into the atmosphere from discarded fridges and air conditioners that were not managed in an environmentally sound manner. This represents approximately 0.3 per cent of the global energy-related emissions in 2019 (Kamiya and Kvarnström 2019, Forti et al. 2020).

Pushing fossil fuel extractionism

Finally, while promising to solve the climate crisis, AI companies are marketing their offers and services to coal, oil and gas companies, thus compromising the efforts to reduce emissions and to divest from fossil fuels. A new report on the future of AI in the oil and gas market published in 2019 by Zion Market Research found that by 2025 the business sector of AI in oil and gas is expected to reach around US$ 4.01 billion globally, growing from 1.75 billion in 2018. Artificial intelligence companies around the world are pushing their capabilities to the oil and gas sectors, promising to increase their efficiencies, optimize their operations and increase productivity: in other words, they are selling their services to increase the pace and productivity of excavation and drilling. Even more alarming are the special oil and gas divisions of digital lords such as Amazon, Google and Microsoft and their partnerships with companies like Chevron, Total, ExxonMobil, Shell and BP (Zion Market Research 2019).

Both Shell and ExxonMobil, for example, signed partnerships with Microsoft Azure in 2018 and 2019 in order to deploy AI programs, while the exploration of oil and gas in Brazil's fragile ecosystem has seen recent employment of AI technology by the state-owned oil giant Petrobras; similarly, the European oil giant Royal Dutch Shell has signed a partnership with the AI company C3 (Joppa and Herweijer 2018).

In 2018, Google started an oil and gas division department with the aim of attracting the fossil fuel industry. The company promised that its machine-learning tools, combined with its cloud service, could help those companies use their data more efficiently and therefore extract oil and gas from existing reserves faster and more powerfully. Amazon is attracting big corporations in the oil and gas industry, with plans that it claims can predict 'the next oil field in seconds with machine learning'. In an internal database of 'oil and gas key accounts', the target clients listed include some of the largest private contributors to climate change, notably ExxonMobil and Chevron, and entities such as Aramco, Saudi Arabia's state-owned oil company (Amazon 2018).

The development of AI technologies has a major impact on the climate crisis. These technologies are supported by material infrastructures and devices that deplete scarce materials and energy resources, generating pollution and waste.

The acceleration of the impact of human interventions on the Earth's ecosystems identified by climate research coincides with the accelerating haste in the development of communication and computational systems (Brevini and Murdock 2017). This has in turn drastically increased our consumption of raw materials and energy, rapidly compounding our global environmental challenges. Facilitated by decades of unregulated capitalism, AI services and products also bear massive responsibility for generating uberconsumerism and destructive hyperconsumption. New developments in AI – especially neural networks – place high demands on energy, while the gains in efficiency currently achieved in data centres have proved very slow in compensating for the escalating demands of computational power.

Even more alarming is that tech giants are involved in highly profitable deals with the biggest energy companies in the world, thus making the 'slow violence' of fossil fuel extraction continuous and relentless.

Conclusion
AI and the Climate Crisis

As I write these lines, the world is still shaken by a global pandemic that has led to millions of deaths and countless chronic illnesses, together with profound social and economic upheaval. While we worry about this public health crisis, we should remember that there is another crisis the planet is facing, linked to the pandemic and not going away: the global climate crisis.

Even during the lockdowns, the reduction in emissions was not significant, as energy consumption kept growing. The status quo is not an option, as we are still burning fossil fuels even during the serious economic recession caused by the pandemic. Without a fundamental shift to renewable resources in global energy production, the economic, social, health and environmental damage of the climate crisis will be far worse than anything we experienced during the pandemic. And further pandemics are likely to emerge, too, as we continually encroach on the natural habitat of wildlife. Without challenging the current mantras of limitless economic growth and boundless consumerism, without reconsidering the way in which the structures, the violence and the inequality of capitalism work, we won't be able to achieve the radical change we need.

For decades, ecological criticism has firmly established that it is the violence and inequality of capitalism that have ultimately caused the ecological emergency we now face (Foster 2001, 2002). Adding to this view, the acceleration of the impact of human interventions on the Earth's ecosystems identified by climate research coincides with an exponentially increasing velocity in the development of communication and computational systems (Brevini and Murdock 2017). This has in turn drastically accelerated our consumption of raw materials and energy, rapidly compounding our global environmental challenges.

As I have argued in this book, AI is being sold as a magic solution. As happened with almost every technology since the Enlightenment, we are being led to believe that it is a panacea for the many ills produced by previous, 'magical' technologies. This absolute faith in techno-solutionism – which is embraced and supported by Silicon Valley's cybertarian circles and by governments all around the world (Dyer-Witheford 1999; Brevini in press) – turns into a powerful justification of the status quo and of the current structure of capitalism, leaving very little room for alternative paths.

'Further pandemics are likely as we continually encroach on the natural habitat of wildlife.'

This book has revealed how AI relies on technology, machines and infrastructure that deplete scarce resources through their production, consumption and disposal, thus devouring a lot of energy and exacerbating the problems of waste and pollution. New developments in AI – especially neural networks – place escalating demands on energy, water and resources in their production, transportation and use, reinforce a culture of hyperconsumerism, and add to the accumulating amounts of waste and pollution already generated by accelerating rates of digital obsolescence and disposal (Gabrys 2013). The efficiency gains currently achieved in data centre sustainability have failed to offset the increasing demands of computational power. Despite some pledges by the tech giants to achieve zero carbon emissions, the reality is that several data centres in the world are still powered by fossil fuels, while zero-net emissions are achieved through calculated systems of carbon credit purchases. Even more alarming is that tech giants such as Microsoft, Google and Amazon are constantly declaring their environmental commitments, while at the backdoor they sign highly profitable deals with the biggest fossil fuel energy companies in the world, the likes of BP, Chevron, Total, ExxonMobil, Shell and Aramco. These deals are designed to increase energy companies' use of AI in fossil fuel extraction, making their work more effective and more violent. Tech giants are helping non-renewable energy companies to automate the drilling and the invasive exploration of previously undeveloped, ecologically fragile, and often sacred First Nation lands, making mineral identification and extraction more 'efficient' than ever.

This book has also shown the myriad connections between big tech and politics, where some of the world's biggest companies are controlling and shaping the debates on AI developments globally.

Returning to the central question of this book – *Is AI Good for the Planet?* – my answer is a resounding 'no'. I have demonstrated how efficient AI is in boosting the systems and technologies of capitalism, thus creating more profit for the wealthiest companies. AI advances productivity and efficiency and reduces labour costs, while the production of AI-enhanced applications in turn advances uberconsumerism and more data extraction. This is especially true of manufacturing, logistics and transport, all of which are labour- and energy-intensive industries. The world's most powerful tech corporations in the West and in China, as we have seen, deploy AI in order to gain incredible competitiveness and to control new markets. This behaviour is reminiscent of the traditional strategies of imperialist colonizers.

Resources to build AI are taken from developing countries that don't have any of the necessary infrastructure, data centres, research centres, or other means to participate fully in, or monitor, the precipitous competition for AI. Furthermore, as this book has shown, very often the same developing countries bear the environmental costs of AI, from the mining of resources necessary to build AI devices to their disposal, thus deepening the inequalities of colonialist capitalism.

Instead of embracing AI as a utopian solution to the world's problems, we should start quantifying and considering the environmental costs and damages of the current acceleration of algorithm-powered AI. As we look to the future, we need to ensure that the alleged benefits of using AI to tackle climate change outweigh the costs. And we need to be able to say 'no' to certain AI applications when their impact on the environment is simply not justifiable.

What can we do?

I would like to conclude by suggesting a few practical strategies and policy recommendations that can help to mitigate the worst effects of AI developments, turning us away from the temptations of consumer sovereignty that place the burden of making sustainable choices only on us, as individuals. Addressing the power asymmetries that current AI development is already displaying necessitates both structural reform and individual behaviour change.

Changing the debate: Participating in public discussions

The first step is to push for a more robust public debate around AI and its detrimental impact on our chances to stop the climate crisis.

The growing concerns and appeals for caution, in Europe, concerning the use of AI in military operations show that it's possible to challenge the dominant discourse on AI. In December 2020, the European Parliament stressed once again that AI systems used for military purposes should be deemed lawful only if subject to human control, allowing humans to correct or disable them in case of unforeseen behaviour. Similar calls for caution were made around the use of AI in matters where human expertise is crucial to safeguarding human rights, for example in public health (e.g. robot-assisted surgery, predictive medicine, smart prosthetics) or in the judiciary (decision-making by judges). As Frank Pasquale astutely notes in his latest book,

Sometimes it will be difficult to demonstrate that a human-centered process is better than an automated one. Crude monetary metrics crowd out complex critical standards. For example, machine learning programs may soon predict, based on brute-force natural language processing, whether one book proposal is more likely than another to be a best seller. From a purely economic perspective, such programs may be better than editors or directors at picking manuscripts or scripts. Nevertheless, those in creative industries should stand up for their connoisseurship. (Pasquale 2020: 5)

The European Parliament also warned about threats to fundamental human rights that arise from the use of AI in mass surveillance, both in the civil and in the military domains. It called for a total ban on highly intrusive social scoring applications, which were introduced by public authorities for monitoring and rating of citizens. The recent bans on the use of AI-powered facial recognition technologies adopted in major US cities such as Portland, Boston and San Francisco are another example of the importance of mobilizing activists, citizens and civil society organizations to engage in acts of resistance on the basis of informed research.

How can we bring about vigorous debate on the unsustainable nature of AI technologies and on their calamitous consequences for the climate crisis? Well, taking advantage of a policy window should be the first step. At the time of writing, there are a number of international agreements, position papers and guidelines that are being discussed, all of them initiated in global fora or at national levels. For example, the Council of Europe is working on a legal framework designed to regulate the use of AI across all forty-seven member states. UNESCO is currently developing a new recommendation on the ethics of artificial intelligence. These are important fora where a discussion on AI and the climate crisis should take place. But at the moment it seems that global discussions on the climate crisis – for example in the context of UN Conferences of the Parties – are yet to address properly the connection between the climate crisis and AI.

Producing more research that is unbiased and objective

More research is needed in order to ascertain the environmental effects of the global production chain of AI. When researchers set out to calculate AI's and tech companies' climate footprint, the first hurdle they have to overcome is how little information is available.

For example, Belkhir and Elmeligi authored a major study where they calculated that the tech industry's carbon footprint could increase to 14 per cent by 2040, 'accounting for more than half of the current relative contribution of the whole transportation sector' (Belkhir and Elmeligi 2018: 1). They lamented a frustrating lack of access to sites and information and its long-lasting consequences for independent research.

As Dobbe and Whittaker (2019) noted, Greenpeace is in agreement (see Greenpeace International 2017). In one of their most recent studies, they report:

> Greenpeace asked tech companies to release straightforward information about data center energy impact, including the size of data center facilities and the percentage of renewables they used. They noted that the 'continued lack of transparency by many companies ... remains a significant threat to the sector's long-term sustainability'. (Dobbe and Whittaker 2019)

So, on the one hand independent researchers struggle to access coherent data from the tech industry, and on the other hand we have too many examples of industry trying to influence research by hiring its own in-house scientists.

As I have discussed in chapters 2 and 3, the recent dismissal of Timnit Gebru from Google after the company attempted to suppress her research casts even more doubt on the ability of scholars hired by the industry to carry out independent research that does not fit the agenda of big tech. Controlling research is just another example of how the tech industry is becoming too influential and impedes independent research.

Adequate research on the environmental costs of AI would need to span its entire production chain, from mineral extractions in developing countries, where such extractions are needed for manufacturing in spite of their harmful and polluting local impact, to the computing energy spent in data centres and cloud systems – and this should encompass the computational costs of data extraction, algorithm training and analysis. It should also focus on the resource depletion caused by the distribution, transportation and post-consumption of material technology; and it should analyse the impact of e-waste and disposal needs.

Demanding transparency

While many corporations now audit the production conditions of subcontractors' factories, often in less developed economies, there is an urgent need for corporations that own clouds and data centres to be accountable. One crucial intervention could be to make it mandatory for server farms and data centres to achieve zero emissions by adopting renewables only, and to cut completely their reliance on fossil fuels. This could be achieved through government regulation that requires mandatory *green certification*.

Despite the proliferating numbers of environment reports developed by tech giants and the existence of zero-carbon emission pledges, information about a tech company's total climate impact is not yet mandatory and is very often obfuscated by non-transparent accounts. As I mentioned earlier in chapter 3, very often tech companies that offset emissions through external funding or credit purchases allow emissions to grow, at a time when the scientific consensus demands that emissions be halved by 2030. A green certification of the total climate footprint of a company should state clearly the impact of its computing cycles, infrastructures, water-cooling systems and other system developments. Such certification should be publicly available and should be calculated in ways that inform customers and platform users on all these topics.

As machine learning and deep learning expand, so will the tech industry's energy needs and carbon footprint, as the previous chapters have amply demonstrated. Hence enforcing regulation that makes transparent the carbon footprint of each specific AI application would certainly be a step in the right direction. Cornell University in New York City has proposed for example the adoption of an energy usage report[1] that should further push green algorithm accountability. Similarly, with the aim of achieving further transparency about the carbon emissions produced by the training of AI models, Mila, a research institute in AI based in Montreal, has developed a Machine Learning Emissions Calculator designed to help AI developers estimate the amount of carbon emissions produced by the training of AI models.[2] Mila also advises developers on how they can reduce emissions by selecting their cloud infrastructure in regions that use lower carbon energy sources.

As AI necessitates more and bigger computing capabilities, measuring the carbon footprint of algorithms and disclosing this information is of paramount importance. However, as discussed in this book, members of the public would need to have a full idea of the carbon footprint of each of the AI-powered systems they use in order to add it to the carbon footprint of the particular device on which the application in question is running. One solution could be to offer a transparent account of the carbon footprint of AI-powered devices in the form of a tech carbon footprint label. The label could provide information on the raw materials used, the carbon costs involved and the recycling options available; this would raise awareness and adequately inform regulators and the public about the implications of adopting each piece of smart technology. How much energy has been used to produce my smart refrigerator, my smart car, my smart vacuum cleaner? How much energy has been required to transport, assemble and deliver the product? How much energy went into developing the machine learning that is now at the core of the applications carried by my smart device? How much energy went into collecting, through ubiquitous data extraction, the data that feed into machine learning? How energy-intensive was the extraction of mineral resources for the manufacture of the device? What is the cost of disposal for these technologies? These are figures that should be made available to policymakers, so that they can make informed decisions, and to the public, so that it can make informed choices.

In 2000, Bill Joy, a co-founder of Sun Microsystems and a huge personality in tech history, surprised Silicon Valley from the columns of *Wired* with an article titled 'Why the Future Doesn't Need Us'. He noted that many of Silicon Valley's dreams would deliberately include the termination of the human species. 'Shouldn't we be asking' Joy wrote, 'how we can best coexist with them? And if our own extinction is a likely, or even possible, outcome of our technological development, shouldn't we proceed with great caution?' (Joy 2000). Twenty years later, in times of climate crisis, these words could not be more prophetic.

Breaking up the digital lords, breaking up data ownership

This book showed how current AI developments are driven by digital lords with unaccountable practices of data accumulation and extractionism; it also showed the centrality of data capitalism in the accelerated turn to AI.

Interventions such as the one proposed by the campaign team of the Democrat candidate Elisabeth Warren could be a first step in the right direction. A stringent application of antitrust laws is vital. And we should equally consider Warren's proposal that large tech platforms be considered 'platform utilities' and barred from owning both the platform utility where participants are competing and any participants on that platform.

These reforms would have the benefit of fragmenting the unchallenged market power of tech giants, while also fragmenting the ownership of data. As I have argued, the digital lords have a massive monopoly on the ownership of data, which gives them a major competitive advantage. A set of policies that reaffirm the right of citizens to retain access to their own data could be a powerful instrument in the fight to regain control and shape the future of AI.

Further policy interventions

Another crucial policy intervention should be to prevent technology obsolescence by requesting manufacturers to lengthen the lifespan of smart devices and to provide spare parts that should replace faulty components.

Bringing green activists and tech workers together to demand action on the climate crisis

In the past two years an unprecedented climate action movement, the movement of secondary school students inspired by Greta Thunberg, has grown into a global network of campaigns focused on systemic change, all aiming to tackle the climate crisis. On 15 March 2019, 1.4 million school pupils filled streets and squares in 112 countries to support Thunberg's call for intergenerational justice and for a liveable future. In September 2019, thousands of employees from Amazon, Google,

Microsoft, Facebook and Twitter, organized as the Tech Workers Coalition, marched to demand their employers reduce their emissions to zero by 2030, to stop exploiting climate refugees, and to cancel contracts with fossil fuel companies. In a very clear statement, the Tech Workers Coalition called out '[t]ech's dirty role in climate change', highlighting that 'the tech industry has a massive carbon footprint, often obscured behind jargon like "cloud computing" or "bitcoin mining", along with depictions of code and automation as abstract and immaterial' (Tech Workers Coalition 2020). These movements, united with the climate justice movement of communities around the world that have been dispossessed of their land, air, water and livelihoods as a result of extractive activities such as mining, fracking and drilling, have a huge potential to bring the climate crisis to the centre of the debate on AI developments. Their example helps to engage many more green citizens and mobilize them to demand climate action. Think for example of the extraordinary achievements of Extinction Rebellion (XR), which in April 2019, within weeks of its first mass mobilization in London, managed to influence public opinion so as to ensure that the UK parliament declare a climate emergency, while the UK government announced a legally binding target for net-zero carbon emissions by 2050.

Green tech literacy

Additionally, global policymaking should support educational programs that enhance *green tech literacy*, educate citizens about the need for more accountability, and raise awareness around the costs of hyperconsumerism and the importance of a responsible energy consumption. Green tech literacy programs should also be implemented in schools as part of curricula, as they promote responsible consumption and tech awareness.

Green tech literacy programs should also contain or encourage interventions to ban products that are too data-demanding and deplete too much energy. The recent request by the EU commissioner to lower the default quality of the video-streaming services offered by Netflix, YouTube and Amazon in order to preserve bandwidth during the coronavirus lockdowns is a good start in this direction.

A final word

As the recent global pandemic crisis has shown, governments around the world can act quickly when urgent action is needed for the public good. We also need to acknowledge the role of environmental damage in causing this and other recent public health crises. And we need to recognize that these and other natural disasters will become more frequent as global warming increases. Embracing a green agenda for a kind of AI that puts the climate crisis at its centre should be our urgent priority. A first step would be to abandon a limited ethical framework, which focuses only on the industry's promise of ethical behaviour, and make it mandatory for it to comply with public policy and public interest.

For what purpose, and with what consequences for collective well-being, should we shape AI? What values should guide its development, if we want to stop the climate crisis? Why does it have to be so difficult to distinguish between socially positive AI applications, which could be developed in an environmentally sustainable way, and AI applications that should not be made at all?

After all, even with his immense belief in science, Stephen Hawking famously stated: 'Success in creating effective AI could be the biggest event in the history of our civilization. It might also be the last, unless we learn how to avoid the risks'.[3]

Notes to Chapter 1

1   In October 1957, the Soviet Union launched the Earth's first
     artificial satellite, Sputnik 1. Historically, this has generated such
     a frenzy of research to compete and conquer the space that the
     United States started investing unprecedented amounts of money
     and eventually touched the Moon. This is where the idea of a
     'Sputnik moment' comes from.

2   'Datafication' is a term that was introduced by Viktor Mayer-
     Schönberger and Kenneth Cukier (2013) in their 2013 book *Big
     Data: A Revolution That Will Transform How We Live, Work,
     and Think*. It refers to the idea that many aspects of our life are
     transformed into data, taking a quantified format that can be
     analysed, then monitored, tracked, reanalysed, and of course
     monetized.

Notes to Chapter 2

1   In this book Zuboff (2019: 87) explains the difference between
     industrial capitalism and surveillance capitalism. Google's
     inventions revolutionized extraction and established surveillance
     capitalism's first economic imperative: extraction. The
     extraction imperative meant that raw material supplies must be
     procured at an ever-expanding scale. Industrial capitalism had
     demanded economies of scale in production, in order to achieve

high throughput combined with low unit cost. In contrast, surveillance capitalism demands economies of scale in the extraction of behavioural surplus.

2 The study lists a number of worrisome projects, from Baltimore's secret use of drones for the daily surveillance of residents to the development, by the Chinese firm ZTE, of Marseille's mass monitoring project Big Data of Public Tranquillity and to the array of surveillance techniques that are deployed at the US–Mexico border.

Note to Chapter 3

1 I'd like to emphasize that this study assessed the energy consumption necessary to train four large neural networks, a type of AI used for processing language. It should be noted that these types of language-processing AI are at the basis of the algorithms that are used for example by Google Translate or Open AI. Of course, the results would be different with other types of machine learning. Although these results cannot be applied to all types of AI, their alarming findings should not be ignored.

Notes to Conclusion

1 On this report, visit https://www.climatechange.ai/papers/neurips 2019/8.

2 For more information on this calculator, visit https://mlco2.git hub.io/impact.

3 Visit https://www.brainyquote.com/quotes/stephen_hawking_62 7109.

Accenture (2019). 'AI: Built to scale'. Accenture website. November 14. https://www.accenture.com/gb-en/insights/artificial-intelligence/ai-investments.

AI Business (2016). 'Google CEO Sundar Pichai: "We will move from mobile first to an AI first world."' https://aibusiness.com/document.asp?doc_id=760029.

Amazon (2018). 'Your guide to AI and machine learning at reinvent 2018'. https://aws.amazon.com/blogs/machine-learning/your-guide-to-ai-and-machine-learning-at-reinvent-2018.

Amazon (2020). 'Carbon footprint'. https://sustainability.aboutamazon.com/environment/sustainable-operations/carbon-footprint.

Arad, B. et al. (2020). 'Development of a sweet pepper harvesting robot'. *Journal of Field Robotics* 37(6): 1027–39.

Asafu-Adjaye, J. et al. (2015). 'An ecomodernist manifesto'. http://www.ecomodernism.org.

Bastani, A. (2017). 'Fully automated green communism'. Novara Media. https://novaramedia.com/2017/11/19/fully-automated-green-communism.

Belkhir, L. and A. Elmeligi (2018). 'Assessing ICT global emissions footprint: Trends to 2040 & recommendations'. *Journal of Cleaner Production* 177: 448–63.

Bender, E. M., T. Gebru, A. McMillan-Major, and S. Shmitchell (2021). 'On the Dangers of Stochastic Parrots: Can Language Models Be Too Big?'. In Proceedings of the 2021 ACM Conference on Fairness, Accountability, and Transparency. New York:

Association for Computer Machinery, pp. 610–623. https://doi.org/10.1145/3442188.3445922.

Benkler, Y. (2019). 'Don't let industry write the rules for AI'. *Nature* 569(7755): 161–162.

Brevini, B. (2020). 'Conclusion'. In *Amazon: Understanding a global communication giant*, by B. Brevini and L. Swiatek. New York: Routledge, pp. 65–70.

Brevini, B. (in press). 'Creating the technological saviour: The myth of artificial intelligence in Europe'. In *AI for everyone?*, edited by P. Verdigen. London: University of Westminster Press.

Brevini, B. and G. Murdock (2017). *Carbon capitalism and communication: Confronting climate crisis*. London: Palgrave Macmillan.

Brevini, B. and F. Pasquale (2020). 'Revisiting the Black Box Society by rethinking the political economy of big data'. *Big Data & Society* 7(2): 1–4.

Brevini, B. and L. Swiatek (2020). *Amazon: Understanding a global communication giant*. New York: Routledge.

Bughin, J. et al. (2018). 'Notes from the AI frontier: Modeling the impact of AI on the world economy'. McKinsey Global Institute. https://www.mckinsey.com/featured-insights/artificial-intelligence/notes-from-the-ai-frontier-modeling-the-impact-of-ai-on-the-world-economy#.

Carey, J. W. (1992) [1989]. *Communication as culture*. New York: Routledge.

Carnegie Endowment for International Peace (2019). *Annual Report, 2019*. https://carnegieendowment.org/about/annualreport/2019.

Chan, M. and L. Zhen (2019). 'Modern military remains top priority as China boosts defence spending'. *South China Morning Post*, 5 March.

'China may match or beat America in AI' (2017). *Economist*, 15 July.

Cimons, M. (2019). 'This robot is delivering coral babies to the Great Barrier Reef'. EcoWatch, 13 January. https://www.ecowatch.com/great-barrier-reef-larvalbot-2625750101.html.

CISCO (2020). 'Cisco annual Internet report (2018–2023)'. White Paper, 9 March. https://www.cisco.com/c/en/us/solutions/collateral/executive-perspectives/annual-internet-report/white-paper-c11-741490.html.

Cognilytica (2020). *Worldwide country AI strategies and competitiveness 2020*. Cognilytica, 7 February. Downloadable from https://www.cognilytica.com/download/worldwide-country-ai-strategies-and-competitiveness-2020-cgr-str20.

Cook, G., E. Jardim, and C. Craighill (2019). 'Clicking clean Virginia: The dirty energy powering Data Center Alley'. Greenpeace. https://www.greenpeace.org/usa/reports/click-clean-virginia.

Crawford, K. and R. Calo (2016). 'There is a blind spot in AI research'. *Nature News* 538(7625): 311–13.

Crawford, K. et al. (2016). 'The AI now report'. *Social and Economic Implications of Artificial Intelligence Technologies in the Near-Term*. https://scholar.google.com/citations?user=ve4ZaJcAAAAJ&hl=en#d=gs_md_cita-d&u=%2Fcitations%3Fview_op%3Dview_citation%26hl%3Den%26user%3Dve4ZaJcAAAAJ%26citation_for_view%3Dve4ZaJcAAAAJ%3AYsMSGLbcyi4C%26tzom%3D-60.

Dadich, S. (2016). 'Barack Obama, neural nets, self-driving cars, and the future of the world'. *Wired*, November. https://www.magzter.com/stories/Science/WIRED/Barack-Obama-Neural-Nets-Self-driving-Cars-and-the-Future-of-the-World.

Debus, P. (2019). 'Al Gore trains climate warriors of the future in Brisbane'. *Mandarin*, 14 June. https://www.themandarin.com.au/109940-al-gore-trains-climate-warriors-of-the-future-in-brisbane.

Dempsey, K. (2017). 'Democracy needs a reboot for the age of artificial intelligence'. *Nation*, 8 November. https://www.thenation.

com/article/archive/democracy-needs-a-reboot-for-the-age-of-arti
ficial-intelligence.

Ding, J. (2019). 'ChinAI #51: China's AI "national team"'. ChinAI
Neswletter, 20 May. https://chinai.substack.com/p/chinai-51-chi
nas-ai-national-team.

Dobbe, R. and M. Whittaker (2019). 'AI and climate change:
How they're connected, and what we can do about it'. AI Now
Institute, 17 October. https://medium.com/@AINowInstitute/
ai-and-climate-change-how-theyre-connected-and-what-we-can-
do-about-it-6aa8d0f5b32c.

Dyer-Witheford, N. (1999). *Cyber-Marx: Cycles and circuits of struggle in high-technology capitalism*. Chicago: University of Illinois
Press.

Elish, M. C. and Boyd, D. (2018). 'Situating methods in the magic of
Big data and AI'. *Communication Monographs* 85(1): 57–80.

Ernst, D. (2020). *Competing in artificial intelligence chips: China's
challenge amid technology war*. Centre for International Governance
Innovation, 26 March. https://www.cigionline.org/publications/
competing-artificial-intelligence-chips-chinas-challenge-amid-tech
nology-war.

European Commission (2018a). 'Communication: Artificial intelligence for Europe'. Shaping Europe's Digital Future. Policy
and Legislation, 25 April. https://digital-strategy.ec.europa.eu/en/
library/communication-artificial-intelligence-europe.

European Commission (2018b). 'EU member states sign up to coop-
erate on artificial intelligence'. Shaping Europe's Digital Future.
Digibyte, 10 April. https://digital-strategy.ec.europa.eu/en/news/
eu-member-states-sign-cooperate-artificial-intelligence.

European Commission (2019a). 'Ethics guidelines for trustworthy
AI'. Shaping Europe's Digital Future. Report Study, 8 April.
https://ec.europa.eu/digital-single-market/en/news/ethics-guide
lines-trustworthy-ai.

European Commission (2019b). 'Policy and investment recommendations for trustworthy artificial intelligence'. Shaping Europe's Digital Future. Report Study, 26 June. https://ec.europa.eu/digital-single-market/en/news/policy-and-investment-recommendations-trustworthy-artificial-intelligence.

European Commission (2020a). 'EU member states join forces on digitalisation for European agriculture and rural areas'. Shaping Europe's Digital Future. Digibyte, 10 April. https://digital-strategy.ec.europa.eu/en/news/eu-member-states-join-forces-digitalisation-european-agriculture-and-rural-areas.

European Commission (2020b). 'White Paper on artificial intelligence: A European approach to excellence and trust'. 19 February. https://ec.europa.eu/info/sites/info/files/commission-white-paper-artificial-intelligence-feb2020_en.pdf.

Evans, R. and J. Gao (2016). 'AI reduces Google data centre cooling bill by 40%'. DeepMind, 20 July. https://deepmind.com/blog/article/deepmind-ai-reduces-google-data-centre-cooling-bill-40.

Forti, V. et al. (2020). *The global e-waste monitor 2020: Quantities, flows, and the circular economy potential.* Bonn, Geneva, and Rotterdam: United Nations University, United Nations Institute for Training and Research, International Telecommunication Union, and International Solid Waste Association. https://www.itu.int/en/ITU-D/Environment/Documents/Toolbox/GEM_2020_def.pdf.

Foster, J. B. (2001). 'Ecology against capitalism'. *Monthly Review* 53(5). https://monthlyreview.org/2001/10/01/ecology-against-capitalism.

Foster, J. B. (2002). 'Capitalism and ecology: The nature of the contradiction'. *Monthly Review* 54(4). https://monthlyreview.org/category/2001/volume-53-issue-05-october-2001.

Foster, J. B. and McChesney, R. W. (2014). 'Surveillance capitalism: Monopoly-finance capital, the military–industrial complex, and the digital age'. *Monthly Review* 66(3). https://monthlyreview.org/2014/07/01/surveillance-capitalism.

Fukuyama, F. (1992). *The end of history and the last man*. New York: Simon & Schuster.

Gabrys, J. (2013). 'Plastic and the work of the biodegradable'. In *Accumulation: The material politics of plastic*, edited by J. Gabrys, G. Hawkins, and M. Michael. London: Routledge, pp. 208–27.

Gandy Jr, O. H. (1989). 'The surveillance society: Information technology and bureaucratic social control'. *Journal of Communication* 39(3): 61–76.

Gates, B. (2020). 'COVID-19 is awful: Climate change could be worse'. GatesNotes: The Blog of Bill Gates, 4 August. https://www. gatesnotes.com/Energy/Climate-and-COVID-19.

Gilder, G. (2000). *Telecosm: How infinite bandwidth will revolutionize our world*. New York: Simon & Schuster.

Goode, L. (2018). 'Life, but not as we know it: AI and the popular imagination'. *Culture Unbound: Journal of Current Cultural Research* 10(2): 185–207.

Google (2019). *Environmental report 2019*. Smart Energy Decisions, 7 October. https://www.smartenergydecisions.com/upload/resear ch_+_reports/google_2019-environmental-report.pdf.

Greenpeace International (2011). 'How dirty is your data? A look at the energy choices that power cloud computing'. Corrected version, 24 May. https://www.greenpeace.org/static/planet4-international-stateless/2011/04/4cceba18-dirty-data-report-greenpeace.pdf.

Greenpeace International (2017). 'Clicking clean: Who is winning the race to build a green Internet?' Downloadable from http://www. clickclean.org/international/en.

Hao, K. (2020). 'We read the paper that forced Timnit Gebru out of Google: Here's what it says'. *MIT Technology Review*, 4 December. https://www.technologyreview.com/2020/12/04/1013294/google-ai-ethics-research-paper-forced-out-timnit-gebru.

Harvey, D. (2005). *The new imperialism*. Oxford: Oxford University Press.

References

Haugeland, J. (1989). *Artificial intelligence: The very idea*. Cambridge, MA: MIT Press.

'How big tech funds the debate on AI ethics' (2019). *New Statesman*, 6 June. https://newstral.com/en/article/en/1128188074/how-big-tech-funds-the-debate-on-ai-ethics.

IEA (2017). *Digitalisation and Energy*. IEA: Paris. https://www.iea.org/reports/digitalisation-and-energy.

IEA (2019). *World energy outlook 2019*. Paris: International Energy Agency.

IEA (2020). 'Data centres and data transmission networks'. https://www.iea.org/fuels-and-technologies/data-centres-networks.

'In the struggle for AI supremacy, China will prevail' (2018). *Economist*, 29 September.

Ingrassia, P., A. Sage, and D. Shepardson (2016). 'How Google is shaping the rules of the driverless road'. Reuters, 16 April. https://www.reuters.com/investigates/special-report/autos-driverless.

IPPC (2018). *Global warming of 1.5 degrees C*. https://www.ipcc.ch/sr15.

Isenhour, C. (2016). 'Unearthing human progress? Ecomodernism and contrasting definitions of technological progress in the Anthropocene'. *Economic Anthropology* 3(2): 315–28.

Jing, M. and S. Dai (2017). 'China recruits Baidu, Alibaba and Tencent to AI "national team"'. *South China Morning Post*, 21 November. https://www.scmp.com/tech/china-tech/article/2120913/china-recruits-baidu-alibaba-and-tencent-ai-national-team.

Jones, N. (2018). 'How to stop data centres from gobbling up the world's electricity'. *Nature* 561(7722): 163–6. https://www.nature.com/articles/d41586-018-06610-y.

Joppa, L. and C. Herweijer (2018). 'How AI can enable a sustainable future'. PricewaterhouseCoopers LLP and Microsoft. https://www.pwc.co.uk/sustainability-climate-change/assets/pdf/how-ai-can-enable-a-sustainable-future.pdf.

References

Joy, B. (2000). 'Why the future does not need us'. *Wired*, 4 January. https://www.wired.com/2000/04/joy-2.

Kamiya, O. and O. Kvarnström (2019). 'Data centres and energy: From global headlines to local headaches?'. International Energy Agency, 20 December. https://www.iea.org/commentaries/data-centres-and-energy-from-global-headlines-to-local-headaches.

Kavlakoglu, E. (2020). 'AI vs machine learning vs deep learning vs neural networks: What's the difference?'. IBM, 27 May. https://www.ibm.com/cloud/blog/ai-vs-machine-learning-vs-deep-learning-vs-neural-networks.

Kommenda, N. (2019). 'How your flight emits as much CO_2 as many people do in a year'. *Guardian*, 19 July.

Kurzweil, J. (1985). 'Artificial intelligence: An ideology for the information society'. Studies in Communication and Information Technology, Working Paper #1, Queen's University Kingston, Ontario.

Lee, K. F. (2018). *AI superpowers: China, Silicon Valley, and the new world order*. Boston, MA: Houghton Mifflin Harcourt.

Lewis, J. (2017). 'Digital desires: Mediated consumerism and climate crisis'. In *Carbon capitalism and communication: Confronting climate crisis*, edited by B. Brevini and G. Murdock. London: Palgrave Macmillan, pp. 57–69.

Lopez, I. (2020). Treeswift's autonomous robots take flight to save forests. Phys.org, 13 October. https://phys.org/news/2020-10-treeswift-autonomous-robots-flight-forests.html.

Lynch, L. and T. Chung (2020). 'E-commerce and mobile money for poverty reduction in China: Lessons for African countries'. Center for Global Development, 21 December. https://www.cgdev.org/publication/e-commerce-and-mobile-money-poverty-reduction-china-lessons-african-countries.

Malm, A. and A. Hornborg (2014). 'The geology of mankind? A critique of the Anthropocene narrative'. *Anthropocene Review* 1(1): 62–9.

Mann, A. (2021). *Food in a changing climate*. Bingley: Emerald Publishing.

Martinez, D. R. et al. (2019). 'Artificial intelligence: Short history, present developments, and future outlook: Final report'. MIT Lincoln Laboratory, 1 January. https://www.ll.mit.edu/r-d/publicati ons/artificial-intelligence-short-history-present-developments-and-future-outlook-0.

Maxwell, R. and T. Miller (2012). *Greening the media*. New York: Oxford University Press.

Maxwell, R. and T. Miller (2015). 'High-tech consumerism, a global catastrophe happening on our watch'. The Conversation, 11 September. https://theconversation.com/high-tech-consumerism-a-global-catastrophe-happening-on-our-watch-43476.

Maxwell, R. and T. Miller (2017). 'Digital technology and the environment: Challenges for green citizenship and environmental organizations'. In *Carbon Capitalism and Communication: Confronting climate crisis*, edited by In B. Brevini and G. Murdock. London: Palgrave Macmillan, pp. 41–55.

Maxwell, R. and T. Miller (2020). *How Green Is Your Smartphone?* London: Polity.

Mayer-Schönberger, V. and K. Cukier (2013). *Big data: A revolution that will transform how we live, work, and think*. Boston, MA: Houghton Mifflin Harcourt.

McKinsey & Company (2017). A future that works: Automation, employment, and productivity. McKinsey Global Institute, January. https://www.mckinsey.com/~/media/mckinsey/featured%20insig hts/Digital%20Disruption/Harnessing%20automation%20for%2 0a%20future%20that%20works/MGI-A-future-that-works-Execu tive-summary.ashx.

Microsoft (2020). 'Microsoft sustainability calculator'. https://app source.microsoft.com/en-us/product/power-bi/coi-sustainability. sustainability_dashboard.

References

Mosco, V. (2004). *The digital sublime: Myth, power, and cyberspace*. Cambridge, MA: MIT Press.

Mosco, V. (2014). *To the Cloud: Big Data in a Turbulent World*. Boulder, CO: Paradigm.

Mosco, V. (2017). The next Internet. In *Carbon Capitalism and Communication: Confronting Climate Crisis*, edited by B. Brevini and G. Murdock. London: Palgrave Macmillan, pp. 95–107.

Murdock, G. and B. Brevini (2019). 'Communications and the capitalocene: Disputed ecologies, contested economies, competing futures'. *Political Economy of Communication* 7(1): 51–82.

Natale, S. and A. Ballatore (2017). 'Imagining the thinking machine: Technological myths and the rise of artificial intelligence'. *Convergence: The International Journal of Research into New Media Technologies* 26(1): 3–18.

Negroponte, N. (1998). 'Beyond digital'. *Wired* 6(12). https://web.media.mit.edu/~nicholas/Wired/WIRED6-12.html.

Nelder, V. J. et al. (2017). *Scientific review of the impacts of land clearing on threatened species in Queensland*. Queensland Government. Brisbane, Queensland. https://www.researchgate.net/publication/318649639_Scientific_Review_of_the_impacts_of_land_clearing_on_threatened_species_in_Queensland.

Nye, D. E. (1994). *American technological sublime*. Cambridge, MA: MIT Press.

OECD (2019). *Artificial intelligence in society*. Paris: OECD Publishing. https://ec.europa.eu/jrc/communities/sites/jrccties/files/eedfee77-en.pdf.

OECD (2020). *Digital economy: Outlook 2020*. Paris: OECD Publishing. https://www.ama.gov.pt/documents/24077/219772/OECD+Digital+Economy+Outlook+2020+%2800000002%29.pdf/c5bbd2e5-f50e-461e-882c-82d4d7db5bdb.

Ong, J. C. and J. V. A. Cabañes (2018). 'Architects of networked disinformation: Behind the scenes of troll accounts and fake news production in the Philippines'. ScholarWorks@ UMass Amherst, 74. https://scholarworks.umass.edu/cgi/viewcontent.cgi?article=10 75&context=communication_faculty_pubs.

Pasquale, F. (2020). *New laws of robotics: Defending human expertise in the age of AI*. Cambridge, MA: Harvard University Press.

Rao, A. S. and G. Verweij (2017). 'Sizing the prize: What's the real value of AI for your business and how can you capitalise?' PricewaterhouseCoopers Australia, 8 September. https://www.pwc. com/gx/en/issues/analytics/assets/pwc-ai-analysis-sizing-the-prize-report.pdf (see also https://apo.org.au/node/113101).

Roach, J. (2020). 'Microsoft finds underwater datacenters are reliable, practical and use energy sustainably'. Innovation Stories, 14 September. https://news.microsoft.com/innovation-stories/project-natick-underwater-datacenter.

Roberts, H. et al. (2019). 'The Chinese approach to artificial intelligence: An analysis of policy and regulation'. *AI & Society* 36: 59–77. https://ssrn.com/abstract=3469784.

Roszak, T. (1986). *The cult of information*. New York: Pantheon.

Schwartz, R. et al. (2019). 'Green AI'. Cornell University, arXiv: 1907.10597v3.

The Shift Project (2019). *Lean ICT: Towards digital sobriety*. Report, March. https://theshiftproject.org/wp-content/uploads/2019/03/Lean-ICT-Report_The-Shift-Project_2019.pdf.

Shirky, C. (2008). *Here comes everybody: The power of organizing without organizations*. New York: Penguin Press.

Srnicek, N. (2017). *Platform capitalism*. Cambridge: Polity.

Statista (2020a). 'Number of smartphones sold to end users worldwide from 2007 to 2021'. https://www.statista.com/statistics/263437/global-smartphone-sales-to-end-users-since-2007.

Statista (2020b). 'Penetration rate of Internet users in China from December 2008 to March 2020'. https://www.statista.com/statistics/236963/penetration-rate-of-internet-users-in-china.

Strubell, E., A. Ganesh, and A. McCallum (2019). 'Energy and policy considerations for deep learning in NLP'. Cornell University, arXiv:1906.02243.

Tech Workers Coalition (2020). Poster. https://techworkerscoalition. org/climate-strike.

Tiku, N. (2020). 'Google hired Timnit Gebru to be an outspoken critic of unethical AI. Then she was fired for it'. *Washington Post*, 23 December. https://www.washingtonpost.com/technology/2020/12/23/google-timnit-gebru-ai-ethics.

Tschandl, P. et al. (2020). 'Human–computer collaboration for skin cancer recognition'. *Nature Medicine* 26(8): 1229–34.

UN Environment Programme (2019). 'Emissions gap report'. 26 November. https://www.unep.org/resources/emissions-gap-report-2019.

United Nations News (2020). 'Carbon dioxide levels hit new record; COVID impact "a tiny blip"', WMO says'. Climate and Environment, 23 November. https://news.un.org/en/story/2020/11/1078322.

UQ News (2020). 'Human–artificial intelligence collaborations best for skin cancer diagnosis'. University of Queensland, 24 June. https://www.uq.edu.au/news/article/2020/06/human-artificial-intelligence-collaborations-best-skin-cancer-diagnosis (also in *Science Daily*, 29 June: https://www.sciencedaily.com/releases/2020/06/200629120229.htm).

Williams, R. (1974). *Television: Technology and cultural form*. London: Fontana.

Williams, R. (1981). 'Communication technologies and social institutions'. In *Contact: Human communication and its history*, edited by R. Williams. London: Thames & Hudson, pp. 226–238.

Williams, R. (1985). *Towards 2000*. Harmondsworth: Penguin.

World Economic Forum (2016). 'The new plastics economy: Rethinking the future of plastics'. Geneva, World Economic Forum, January. http://www3.weforum.org/docs/WEF_The_New_Plastics_Economy.pdf.

World Economic Forum (2019). 'How much data is generated each day?' World Economic Forum and Visual Capitalist, 17 April. https://www.weforum.org/agenda/2019/04/how-much-data-is-generated-each-day-cf4bddf29f.

World Economic Forum, with PwC and Stanford Woods Institute for the Environment (2018). 'Harnessing artificial intelligence for the Earth'. January. http://www3.weforum.org/docs/Harnessing_Artificial_Intelligence_for_the_Earth_report_2018.pdf.

World Intellectual Property Organization (2020). 'China becomes top filer of international patents in 2019 amid robust growth for WIPO's IP services, treaties and finances'. WIPO, Geneva, 7 April. https://www.wipo.int/pressroom/en/articles/2020/article_0005.html.

Wu, J. (2020). 'Intel & Accenture use AI to save the coral reef'. *Forbes*, 22 April. https://www.forbes.com/sites/cognitiveworld/2020/04/22/intel--accenture-use-ai-to-save-the-coral-reef/?sh=23a409c05e60.

Yang, T. et al. (2017). 'Developing reservoir monthly inflow forecasts using artificial intelligence and climate phenomenon information'. *Water Resource Research* 53(4): 2786–812.

Zhang, W. (2020). 'The AI girlfriend seducing China's lonely men'. Sixth Tone, 7 December. https://www.sixthtone.com/news/1006531/the-ai-girlfriend-seducing-chinas-lonely-men.

Zhu, R. et al. (2020). 'Hydrological responses to the future climate change in a data scarce region, Northwest China: Application of machine learning models'. *Water* 11(8). https://www.mdpi.com/2073-4441/11/8/1588/htm.

Zion Market Research (2019). 'Global AI in oil and gas market'. Intrado GlobeNewswire, 18 July. https://www.globenewswire.com/news-release/2019/07/18/1884499/0/en/Global-AI-In-Oil-and-Gas-Market-Will-Reach-to-USD-4-01-Billion-By-2025-Zion-Market-Research.html.

Zuboff, S. (2019). *The age of surveillance capitalism: The fight for a human future at the new frontier of power*. London: Profile Books.

Index